TRAILER TRASH, WITH A GIRL'S NAME

STACEY ROBERTS

ISBN: 0615933882
ISBN 13: 9780615933887

TABLE OF CONTENTS

DEDICATION

THIS BOOK IS dedicated to my mother, Carol Glazer Roberts Davidson Schwartman, who had to be both father and mother to me, and did both jobs well. She has inspired me in every aspect of my life. This book shows how she did it.

ACKNOWLEDGEMENTS

BEFORE I WAS a writer, I thought writing was a solitary activity. I believed I would hermit myself in a cave and shun all human contact while I hammered out my book like a lump of iron in a fiery forge. Then I would publish it. Alone.

Wrong.

I figured out soon enough that it takes a community to write a book, from the earliest supporters of the Trailer Trash blog, all the way to the long suffering readers of my roughest drafts, and to final editing and publication.

I begged and pleaded for help with this, my first novel, and I always got more than I asked for. Some of the people who were instrumental in bringing these memoirs out of the trunk:

Mark Gosson, my partner in crime (and writing and business) since we were 14. He got to witness many of the events in the book, and put his immense talent into the design of the cover. He has an uncanny knack of seeing the future, and this collection was part of it.

CF Winn, my fearless, nagging editor, who took these stories the way they came and made them better. She also repossessed most of the commas I tried to use and developed an unhealthy antagonism for dashes.

Maura Stone, scion of a great American comedy family and an early fan of the Trailer Trash blog. I learned what funny truly meant from this great humorist, satirist, and generous artisan.

Clive Johnson, a wordsmith of unparalleled acumen, and coiner of the phrase "madder than a box of frogs." His early enthusiasm for Trailer Trash is a major reason why you are reading this book.

Donna Cavanagh, founder of HumorOutcasts.com. If anyone knows funny, it's her.

Laura Heil, first reader, who read these stories hot (or not so hot) off the presses. If she didn't laugh out loud while reading, I knew I hadn't done my best.

Mary Paddock, Charity Parkerson, Dionne Lister, Amber Jerome-Norrgard, Justin Bogdanovitch, Ben Ditmars, Scott Morgan, Monica La Porta, Javier Robayo, Susan Ilene, Ciara Ballintyne, Alexandria Szeman and countless other writers who inspire me with their limitless talent.

Suzanne Shearer, who believed in these stories even when my own faith in them had disappeared. She helped me see them in a new light when I needed to and motivated me to keep going.

Layne Roberts, who rode along on the early adventures. Winnebagos make for some stressful living. I'm glad we didn't kill each other.

Caitlyn and Erin Roberts, who teach me every day that humor doesn't need to be loud or obvious. Their subtle wit is the guidepost for my funny writing, as they themselves are my inspiration for most everything.

These stories were inspired by my family and friends from childhood, without whom I would not be the man I am today. My deepest thanks to the ghosts of the past, and those who are still here.

FOREWORD

By Donna Cavanagh

A WHILE BACK, I had the privilege of meeting Stacey Roberts. As with many friendships these days, our meeting was not in person, but rather a humorous encounter of the virtual kind that only social media could provide. Although millions of people use the moniker *"writer"* these days, the literary world is still a small one where one *"writer"* friend introduces you to another, you return the favor, and the online support system thrives. I met Stacey through several contacts, and because I'm a humorist myself, I was curious about his work.

We both participated in a podcast, and I found him to be charming and witty. Afterwards, we performed the obligatory "follow backs" and "friending" and I asked if I could read some of his stuff. He led me to his blog, "Trailer Trash, With A Girl's Name," and I quickly became a fan. I invited him to join my site, HumorOutcasts.com, and we quickly began Facebooking, tweeting, networking — the things writers must do these days to survive. When Stacey told me about his upcoming book, I was excited. In a style all his own, and for anyone who was brave enough to click on his page to see, Stacey Roberts invited us into his private thoughts about his life; a life that began with a perceived handicap: a girl's name.

He introduced us to real life characters that affected his existence from the moment of his birth and made him the man we know and love today. Any therapist will tell you that we all have dysfunctional families, but I often thought that Stacey's might set a record if his tales are true.

Every post let us in on the many people who came in and out of his life, and despite their obvious foibles, he still managed to make us like them and at times pity them. He led us down a path that shows us that we are all human, and while some of us have more flaws than others, we still have at least one redeeming quality that says, "Hey, it's okay to like me."

Although I laughed out loud through much of this book, I sometimes wished I could have given Stacey a hug and said, "Damn, you are a good sport." From living on the road in a Winnebago to a laundry list of why he should never marry shiksas with big boobs, I discovered a sensible and strong Stacey Roberts who never gives up.

Viewing his life from a distance, I can honestly see where and how Stacey's keen sense of humor developed. From his most tragic moments in childhood, his sibling grievances, and his worst embarrassments, he forged his personality and direction in life. Sure, Stacey's mom was no June Cleaver, but if there was anyone around to give her sons some strength, it was this woman who had no qualms about pointing out that they didn't have to follow the path of those "sons of bitches" who crept in and out of their lives. Somewhere Stacey learned that lesson, and we are all glad he did.

Donna Cavanagh is a humor entrepreneur and founder of HumorOutcasts.com and HumorOutcasts Press/Shorehouse Books. Cavanagh began her business as a small venture to offer writers a forum to showcase their work in a world that offered few avenues for humor. Ironically, HumorOutcasts.com quickly became a comedy conglomerate featuring the creative talents of over 80 aspiring and accomplished writers, filmmakers, illustrators and comics. Today HumorOutcasts.com is the "go to" site for eclectic comedy and humor. From a "G" to a "just might make you blush" rating, there's something for everyone. Maybe *that's why people keep coming back. As a writer herself, Cavanagh can't stop the humor. A veteran journalist who detoured into humor writing, her books and stories have earned her an international audience and national acclaim. A USA Books Contest finalist (Life On The Off Ramp), Cavanagh's latest book <u>A Canine's Guide to the Good Life</u> was penned with her dogs, which as you might imagine was no small feat (or should we say "paws"?). Host of BlogTalk's HumorOutcasts Radio, she is also a publisher at UR Business Network and host of their show "Write Out Loud". She is also the author of <u>Try and Avoid the Speed Bumps</u>.*

1

HOW I GOT A GIRL'S NAME

AFTER FOUR DECADES, I have come to terms with it. I have a girl's name.

I spent much of my childhood trying to figure out two things:

1. How did I get stuck with it?
2. What should I change it to as soon as I possibly can?

Right around puberty, I decided that the second item was way more important than the first. I needed the manliest of man names to go with my deepening voice and sudden werewolf-like hairiness. I hoped that if I came up with the right one, my mother would finally give in and say, "That's it! Perfect! Let's go to the courthouse and get that thing switched right over."

But she had an answer for every suggestion I made:

1. Dirk Steel (Too metallic)
2. Duke Rottweiler (That's a dog's name)
3. Wolfgang Hammerstrike (That's a wolf's name)
4. Gunnar Ironcannon (We're not Vikings)
5. Layne (That's your brother's name. What is *wrong* with you?)

My mother tried to be supportive.

Mom: "SSSSSStace, there are lots of men named Stacey."

Me: "Name five."

Mom: "Stacy Keach."

Me: "Name four more."

Mom: "Stacy Keach."

Me: "There are five billion people on the planet, Ma," I said. "Half are men. How about even one more?"

Mom (teeth gritted): "SSSSSSSStacy Keach."

My mother never even really explained why she named me Stacey. The closest I ever got to a reason was, "I thought you were gonna die."

***

SOUTH PLAINFIELD, NEW Jersey, circa January, 1971. My mother stubbed out her last pre-natal cigarette. A tired nurse walked on soft-soled shoes into the emergency waiting room at Muhlenberg Hospital.

Sheila the Nurse: "Mrs. Roberts, we can take you back now."

Mom: "The baby's too early. It's gonna die."

Sheila the Nurse: "Now, now. We don't know that for sure."

***

I WAS AT least two months early. If I had come on my original due date, I would have been born around the same day as Layne the Favorite. That would have been a real time saver:

Me: "When do I get to have a birthday party?"

Mom: "You just did."

Me: "That was Layne's party."

Mom: "SSSSSSStace. It was a party on your birthday. Why are you always complaining?"

Me: "He got all the presents."

* * *

BACK IN 1971, my mother walked slowly down the hallway of the hospital, her nurse beside her, holding her by the arm.

Mom: "What's your name?"

Sheila the Nurse: "Sheila."

Mom: "That's nice. Do you have children?"

Sheila the Nurse shook her head.

Mom: (diving right in) "You HAVE been married, haven't you?"

Sheila the Nurse: "No, I haven't."

Mom stopped short and looked Sheila the Nurse up and down, her lips pursed. This was her classic look of contempt. Sometime during the Reagan presidency she added little half-moon glasses she could peer over disdainfully, completing the look.

Mom: "How did THAT happen?"

* * *

BY THE TIME of my wedding in 1993, both my mother and my father had each been married four times. My dad, at the ceremony, suggested that he and my mother should just re-up with each other and make it five. At that time, Mom was married to Marvin, King of the Jews. He did not warm to the idea.

Me: "Marvin, my dad just said the weirdest thing."

Marvin, King of the Jews: "That son of a bitch." (This was my mother's pet name for my father)

Me: "Well, it turns out he's been married four times, and Mom's been married four times, so he thought —"

Marvin, King of the Jews: "You know he asked your mutha to dance?"

Me: "That's sweet. Parents should dance at their kids' weddings. Anyway — he's been married four times, and she's been married four times —"

Marvin, King of the Jews: "Sweet? Do you know what an insult that was to me?"

Me: "I'm sure he would have asked you to dance after he and Mom were done. Soooo, he's been married four times, and she's been married four times —"

Marvin, King of the Jews: "She's STILL married!"

Me: "Everyone knows, Marvin. So he thought it would be a good idea if they just got married to each other for the fifth time! Funny, right?"

Me: "Wow, your face is really red right now."

Me: "That's some eye twitch you got there. Are you winking, or having a stroke?"

Me: "You totally crushed that wineglass you were holding. There's a big chunk of glass stuck in your palm. Let me get some help."

My bride was an emergency medical technician, so I went to tell her that Marvin, King of the Jews, was hemorrhaging. Neither of us had eaten yet, even though it was our wedding day, so she was not in a good mood. Between the emergency patching up of Marvin, King of the Jews and the guilt that came from having both Jewish and Catholic guests at the wedding (we had to stop and see all of them), neither of us got so much as one bite of the expensive dinner our parents had fought over:

Mom: "SSSSStace. This place where the wedding is. They better have a kosher meal, Buster. You know we have to have kosher. Kosher!"

After nearly two decades of watching my family eat cheeseburgers and patronize restaurants that did not stringently follow the Old Testament Cookbook, I figured kosher was way less important than, say, the open bar. But I played along and talked to the wedding planner, Mike.

Me: "Mike. As I may have mentioned, there is a horde of angry Jews expected to attend the wedding. Their queen has demanded a kosher meal be added to the menu."

I had a note my mother had sent along for this meeting. I opened it.

It said:
FISH!
Your Mother

Me: "Perhaps fish?"

Mike the Wedding Planner: "We can do fish."

Me: "Huzzah!"

There was now a choice between grilled halibut and London broil on the menu. All of the Catholics ate the fish and the Jews ate the London broil. The bride and groom ate nothing, although we had consumed a large quantity of soothing brown liquor. Later that night, after leaving the reception, where all the food was, we had to go to a 7-11 convenience store and get some cheese and cold cuts for our wedding dinner.

Although undernourished and under the influence, thanks to the bride, Marvin, King of the Jews did not bleed to death.

Kim: "What the hell happened?"

Me: "He crushed the wineglass he was holding."

Kim: "What is it with you Jews and breaking glass at weddings?"

Me: "It's not a religious thing. I think he's mad because my dad didn't want to dance with him."

She sprang into action. Marvin, King of the Jews told her the whole sordid tale while she fashioned a pressure bandage from a linen napkin and plucked glass shards out of his hand with some tweezers that she borrowed from Skanky Bridesmaid Number Two.

As it turned out, my mother and father did not remarry each other. My broken home endures.

***

CIRCA 1971, MY mother and Sheila the Nurse waited for a doctor. Sheila the Nurse made her as comfortable as possible.

Mom: "I don't know why I can't smoke in here."

Sheila the Nurse: "The doctor will be here any minute. Are you still having contractions?"

Mom: "I keep telling you. SSSSSSSStephanie —"

Sheila the Nurse: "Sheila."

Mom: "SSSSSSSSStella. Listen. The baby's not cooked. You know what happens when a baby's not cooked all the way? Their organs don't grow. Their cells don't form properly. It's not good."

Sheila the Nurse: "The baby's only a couple of months early."

Mom: "SSSSSSSarah. Are you listening to me? It's got no lungs. Do you think a baby can live without lungs?"

Sheila the Nurse: "Let's just wait and see what the doctor has to say. Is your husband on his way?"

Mom: "That son of a bitch? No way. He's probably playing the ponies somewhere."

Sheila the Nurse: "Do you want to call him?"

Mom: "What for? He's not gonna wanna come see the baby. It's gonna die. No lungs. SSSSSSShirley. How long you been a nurse?"

Sheila the Nurse: "Seventeen years."

Mom: "Is that so? Gimme the phone."

She called my Aunt Sissy, who was at home babysitting Layne the Favorite while my mother was at the hospital.

Mom: "Sis. Yeah. How's Layne?"

Mom: "Of course he misses me. I'm his mother."

Mom: "No. It's gonna die. It hasn't got any lungs."

Mom: "Sis. It's not cooked all the way. Its organs aren't formed. How come no one understands that? This is a shitty hospital. It's disgusting. SSSSharon. Why is this hospital so shitty?"

Mom: "What did Layne eat for dinner? Are you keeping him clean? He hates to be dirty. Just bring him here."

Sheila the Nurse: "I don't think this is the best place for your other child."

Mom: "SSSSSSally. Listen. He's my son. He should be with his mother. Sis - just bring him. Ow. This thing hurts. Selma. What the hell is this?"

Sheila the Nurse: "Contractions."

Mom: "Contractions? I never heard of this *facochta* contractions."

Sheila the Nurse: "Didn't you say you have another child?"

Mom (smiling wistfully): "Yes. Layne. He's such a good boy."

Sheila the Nurse: "Is he adopted?"

Mom: "Adopted? No way! He's mine! How can you say such a thing?"

Sheila the Nurse: "Was he delivered by a stork?"

Mom: "A stork? What are you talking about? Ow. What the hell is going on? Get this thing out of me."

Sheila the Nurse: "You didn't have any pain at all with your other child?"

Mom: "Not a bit. I told you, Sheera. There's something wrong with this one. I think it's trying to eat my lungs because it doesn't have any of its own."

Sheila the Nurse: "So maybe it's not going to die if it has the strength to eat your lungs."

Mom: "It hates me."

Sheila the Nurse: "Oh, good. Your doctor's here."

I weighed two pounds, three ounces. I was cleaned up, swaddled, and plopped straightaway into the incubator.

Mom: "What good is that gonna do? Is it gonna grow his lungs back? His organs? His cells?"

Sheila: "Yes. Yes it will."

Mom: "Suzanne. Let me ask you a question. Did you go to nursing school in this country?"

Sheila the Nurse (wheeling my incubator out of the room): "He'll be in the ICU if you want to come see him. He may be there for awhile."

Mom: "My sister is bringing my son to stay with me until I can go home."

Sheila the Nurse: "Do you want to name him? We should put something on the card other than *Baby Boy Roberts.*"

Mom: "Oh, sure. Right. What was your name again?"

Sheila: "Sheila."

Mom: "All right, then. I'll name him that. Suzie's a nice name."

Sheila: "He's a boy."

Someone from the hospital records office brought the form to the room for her to fill out. My father wasn't there, so she filled out his part too. Later, I'll be glad that it doesn't say: *FATHER: Son of a Bitch.*

My mom got stuck on *NAME*:

Records Orderly (with a smile): "Trying to decide?"

Mom: "No. I'm trying to remember that nurse's name."

Records Orderly: "You mean Sheila?"

Mom: "Right. I knew it was something like that." She wrote on the official State of New Jersey form:

TRAILER TRASH, WITH A GIRL'S NAME

STACEY

***

I CAME HOME from the hospital two months later. Because of Layne the Favorite's second birthday, no great fuss was made over me. I didn't know any better, so I cooperated: I was quiet, probably because my lungs weren't fully cooked, and unlike my brother, I was content to lay in my own filth.

As I got older, I grew less cooperative. I was so angry about my name. I'm sure I would have been happier with the hospital's original plan for me - BABY BOY. Would I have gotten teased any less? Doubtful. But with a name like that, maybe I could have had a career as a rapper or a 1920's gangster. Do banks still get robbed with tommy guns, or do I have to do it 21st-century style, where I hack in and steal a penny from every account in the bank? If that's the case, I guess it wouldn't matter if my name was Suzie. Or Sheila.

To this day, I still let my mind wander, thinking of good, strong, manly names. Names that make me sound taller and less doughy, with a firm, resolute hairline and a stunning anatomy.

If my children had been boys, I would have given them right and proper names, that's for sure:

"Hawkwing McKiller Roberts, you stop playing with those dolls right now!" or "Stonecrusher Flint Roberts, don't let that kid take your toy from you. Knock her teeth out! They're just the first set anyway!"

As it turned out, I had girls. I knew just what to do. I gave them girl's names.

2

A BASTARD'S THANKSGIVING...
WITH A SIDE OF GRAVY

Uncle George was a bastard. I knew this because my mother always called him one, and she was specific with titles. My Uncle Stuart was a drinker, her business partner was a schmuck, and my father was a son of a bitch. Her business partner was never a son of a bitch, and my father was never a drinker, even when he drank. I could never aspire to be a schmuck, no matter how hard I tried. Uncle George was pigeonholed: once a bastard, always a bastard.

I even asked my mother: "Why can't Daddy be a bastard?"

Mom: "Because he's a son of a bitch." Done. She was the FDA of human frailty - whatever was wrong with you, she knew it, and gave you a label.

Me: "So what am I?"

Mom: "You're just like your father."

Me: "So I'm a son of a bitch?"

Mom: "Go to bed."

Uncle George the Bastard wasn't a dictionary definition bastard - his parents were married - they were Irish Catholic and probably promised to each other at age five. He was the other kind of bastard, the colloquial kind, who despised bitches, niggers, spics, dogs, cats, kids, hebes, and my grandma.

He spoke only after long silences and thought good parenting was striking any misbehaving kid with whatever he could lay his hands on. You didn't pee in his pool and you didn't sit in his chair. You didn't think for one second that your favorite TV show could possibly preempt whatever he was watching. You rode in the back seat of whatever he drove and when he told you to go fetch that thing over there and bring it back to him, you didn't ask him, "Which thing over where?" unless you wanted to wake up sixty seconds later on the ground; you brought over all you could carry as fast as you could.

He had been a police sergeant when my father was on the force, back in the 1950's, a decade and a half before they each met and married Jewish sisters. Uncle George the Bastard was the one who packed up my father's shit when my mother threw him out of the house.

My mother had called her sister in a rage.

Mom: "Sis, that son of a bitch. Send George over here to pack up his shit and put it out on the curb. Sssssssssssssssss."

She added a long hissing sibilant to the end of her words so you knew she was mad or making a point.

At this point, my Aunt Maxine (Sissy to everyone) did not do a number of things: She did not ask what Fred had done this time. She did not protest that George and Fred had been best friends since the Second World War. She did not say that George was busy eating, watching TV, beating one of his kids, degrading my grandmother, or complaining about Gerald Ford. She put down her quilting and pressed the phone to her breast.

Aunt Sissy (looking at Uncle George the Bastard): "George. Carol wants you to put Fred's shit out on the curb."

He looked back at her, his watery Irish blue eyes cold, falling into one of his deadly silences like an archer pulling back the drawstring on a bow. Sissy stared at him with coal black eyes and an implacable face only two generations removed from icy Polish farmland.

Aunt Sissy: "George. Just go now."

I don't know how Uncle George the Bastard felt about siding with family over his best friend, but he must have gone. My father's shit did indeed hit the curb in 1976. I watched from the window, my mother standing behind me, her arms folded, her lips pursed.

Me: "Mom, what's Uncle George doing?"

Mom: "Putting your father's shit out on the curb. That son of a bitch."

Me: "Why is his shit going out to the curb?"

Mom: "Because I'm not having it in this house anymore."

My mother never answered the question being asked - she made it sound like we were out of room to store things or that my father's golf clubs and underpants were toxic and slowly killing us all.

I asked "why the curb" because the back porch was closer, which would have made the job easier on Uncle George the Bastard. Apparently the use of the curb was part of some kind of 1970's divorce ritual as stringent as leaning left at Passover or the wine-to-bread ratio of a Catholic mass. There was a system:

Step 1: Put the offender's belongings on the curb.

Step 2: Change the locks.

Step 3: Leave a note:

Fred,

Your shit is on the curb.

You're a real son of a bitch.

Carol

Step 4: Reassure the children.

Mom: "Layner, I've put your father's shit on the curb."

Step 5: Turn the children against the missing parent.

Layne the Favorite: "That son of a bitch."

As a practical matter, it meant my father had to drive up our long driveway, go to the back porch, try his key, curse, read the note, hurl more expletives, drive back down to the street, collect his shit, swear eternal vengeance upon my mother, and depart.

Our street was a busy two lane road, so he had to park along the curb with his emergency flashers on so cars would detour around him while he packed up his shit. I'm sure more than one man driving by that scene felt some sympathy for him:

Anonymous New Jersey Man: "Oh, hell. His shit's on the curb. That poor son of a bitch."

**

UNCLE GEORGE THE Bastard was the king of Thanksgiving in 1980. He had retired after twenty years on the force and moved his family from Cranford, New Jersey, a mile from my house, to a farm in the Endless Mountains of Pennsylvania, which was four hours away. That year was the first Thanksgiving we spent with them. Not sure why we couldn't do it when the drive didn't require pee stops, but I wasn't in charge of anything at all until the early nineties, and then for maybe three days before I got married.

That Thanksgiving was the first time I ever had gravy. Can a good gravy change your life? This one did. Jews should reconsider gravy. We don't use it for anything. It's made from meat drippings and a thickening agent. It's something you would normally throw away that instead gets resurrected and used. If we Jews had put gravy on trial before we pitched it out, it would be Jesus. In the genteel cold war between our religion and that of the Goyim, gravy is Easter. It is nowhere close to what God had in mind when He freed us from slavery in Egypt to wander the desert, eat flat crackers, and wait a dozen centuries for the Cossacks to storm down from the hills and pee in our wells.

My mother can't cook, and knows God is okay with that. If He thought His Chosen could prepare food properly, why all the dietary restrictions? Instead of saying, "Undercooked pork can kill you, so do it right," He ordered, "No pork." It implies a lack of confidence in our culinary talents. He could have said, "Cook two cubits of pork over a dry fire for five minutes." Whatever a cubit is.

So, no pork. My mother is food obsessed, and believes herself to be a great Talmudic scholar in pursuit of the Lord's plan. At my wedding, she ruled that there must be a kosher meal. The wedding planner offered fish. My mother agreed. All fish is kosher, she informed me, so we were good.

During my first Thanksgiving on the farm, I noticed my cousins passing around a weird porcelain boat.

Me: "What's that?"

Cousin David: "Gravy."

Me: "What do you put it on?"

Cousin David: (dreamily) "Everything."

I took the gravy boat.

Mom (catching my eye): "SSSSSSSSSSStace. Don't eat that crap."

Me: "But it has its own special dish!"

We Jews love that sort of thing. Passover has its own segmented dish. Wine goes in special cups at Bar Mitzvahs. This gravy boat must have been a relic of one of the lost tribes of Israel, so I brought it back into the fold, covering turkey, stuffing, potatoes, corn, and cranberry sauce with it.

My brother, Layne the Favorite, obediently choked his food down dry. I was so covered in gravy I needed a bath when I was done. I asked my Aunt Sissy, who I now believed to be the world's best cook, what was in her spectacular stuffing, which was so unlike any I had ever had.

Her face got bright red.

Aunt Sissy (through clenched teeth): "Nothing special."

My mother, who never ate stuffing, looked at me wide-eyed.

Mom: "SSSSSStace. It's stuffing. It's bread. What's wrong with you?"

My aunt hustled me from the table to scrub the gravy from my hair and shoes.

Aunt Sissy (whispering): "There's pork sausage in the stuffing. If your mother knew she would just kill me. Or give me a title. Sissy the Corrupter. Something like that. You know how she is."

Me: "It's got a nice ring to it. I think I've got gravy in my belly button."

Aunt Sissy: "I'm not gonna risk it over a side dish." She wiped away a glob of gravy from the back of my left knee.

Me (also whispering and horrified): "But Grandma eats the stuffing. She loves it." Grandma was very religious.

Aunt Sissy: "Grandma eats lobster too."

Everything I knew about the book of Exodus hit me like a brick made from Nile river mud.

Me: "Lobster's not kosher..."

Aunt Sissy: (shrugging) "Nope. How did you get gravy in your ears?"

Me: "You ARE a corrupter! Can you teach my mother to cook?"

Aunt Sissy: "No. No one can."

Aunt Sissy: "Why are you crying? It's just a little spilled gravy."

3

THE CROWN PRINCE

I⊤ was a strategy that was doomed to fail. Like Hannibal crossing elephants over the Alps or Philip II's Spanish Armada - it really should have worked.

In every house there is a favorite child, often the firstborn, who gets the best stuff first: toys, privileges, cars. He or she sits at the right hand of their parents. It is a tradition dating back to the Old Testament, when God's chosen people lived in the desert, herded goats, and spoke to Him as if He was just some guy you hung around with. Right up until He commanded you to kill your own son or build an ark so He could wipe out all life on earth, including all but two of your favorite goats.

I was not the son of choice. Layne the Favorite got all the perks in our house. It stood to reason that if I stuck close to him, some of that largesse would find its way to me, like trickle-down economics.

In my defense, I conceived of this plan when I was five.

***

LAYNE THE FAVORITE's bedtime was at least half an hour later than mine. For a stretch of years I like to call The Great Injustice, it was a whole hour and a half - me at seven thirty, him at nine o'clock. This was during the time immediately following the divorce, which began shortly after the nation's bicentennial.

Me: "So what do we do now?"

Mom: "You're going to bed."

Me: "But it's only seven thirty! What about him?"

Mom: "You just worry about yourself, Mister."

Me: "I am!"

Mom: "Move it!"

So there I was, in bed while it was still daylight, listening to the sounds of my friends outside getting a few frantic last minutes of playing in while their parents howled their names from upstairs windows.

At eight o'clock I heard the TV in the next room click on and the theme from *Rhoda* start up. It seemed my mother was going to console herself by watching sitcoms with strong female leads, her son at her side. Half an hour later was *Mary Tyler Moore*. I was steaming mad by then.

I hopped out of bed and padded in my scratchy footie pajamas to the living room, where the two of them sat side by side, munching popcorn.

Me: "Popcorn? We never get popcorn!"

Mom: "SSSSStace. What is wrong with you?"

Me: "For one thing, I'm in bed at seven thirty."

Mom: "You're not in bed." Munch, munch.

Layne the Favorite: "It's not seven thirty." Munch, munch.

Great. Now they were masters of logic.

Me: "Why does he get to stay up late and watch TV?"

Mom: "SSSSStace. Listen. His father and I are getting divorced. It affects him."

Me: "Doesn't it affect me?"

Mom: "Of course not. You have to understand. He's sssssssensitive."

Me: "I'm sensitive! Whatever that is."

Mom: "No you're not. You're just like your father."

Layne the Favorite: "That son of a bitch."

Mom: "Go to bed." Munch, munch.

I got sent to bed at seven thirty the next night. Friday.

Me: "But it's Friday! It's seven thirty!"

Mom: "SSSSSStace. I have a watch."

This was utterly incomprehensible.

Me: "What does that mean?"

Mom: "You're always telling me what time it is. I have a watch. You're not doing me any favors. Just go to bed."

Eight o'clock. I could hear the sounds of popcorn being munched and the jazzy music of the *Sanford and Son* theme. I'd had it. I got out of bed, stripped off my footie pajamas, and stalked naked to the living room. I folded my arms and stood blocking the TV.

Mom: "Are you naked?"

I said nothing.

Layne the Favorite: "Get out of the way."

Mom: "SSSSStace. Why don't you have any clothes on?"

Me: "Because I'm sensitive!"

My ploy failed. I got sent back to bed. But to this day, if you want to get my clothes off, play the *Sanford and Son* theme. Works every time.

It was during one of these TV watching sessions that Layne made his big move.

Layne the Favorite: "You know how sensitive I am. And that the divorce is reflecting me."

Mom: "Affecting you, honey."

Layne the Favorite: "Right. So I was thinking about what would make me feel less infected."

Mom: "Affected."

Layne the Favorite: "I think a new bike would really help. With my being deflected."

Mom: "That's a great idea!"

I bolted into the living room and stood in front of the TV, buck-ass naked.

Me: "You have GOT to be kidding me!"

She bought the bike the next day and promptly called my father. Layne the Favorite and I sat and listened to her end of the conversation.

Mom: "Fred. Listen. I bought your son a bike. You need to come over and put it together."

Mom: "No way, Fred. I wasn't going to have the damn store put it together. They wanted seven bucks! That's highway robbery. Disgusting."

Mom: "Not like you'd give me the seven bucks. You can't even pay my sssssstinkin child support."

Mom: "Just get over here and put this thing together. Son of a bitch."

It took my dad all day and one hundred and eleven curse words to put the bike together. He had a number of things working against him:

1. No talent for mechanical things (which I inherited).
2. He chain smoked, and was building the bike with one hand.
3. White hot anger for my mother made his remaining hand shake. He kept dropping the smaller bits of bike, which I dutifully retrieved.

At least until seven thirty.

Mom: "SSSSSStace. Time for bed."

Dad: "Bed? It's Saturday. And it's only seven thirty!"

Mom: "I've got a goddamned watch, Fred!"

Dad: "What?"

Mom: "You think he should stay up later?"

Dad: "At least on the weekends. And why should Layne stay up later than him?"

Mom: "He needs his rest. Otherwise he's like a crazy person. He has all kinds of strange ideas running around in his head. He thinks we should eat gravy. Gravy!"

Dad: "He's a weird little guy."

Mom: "He's just like you."

It took another hour for the bike to be ready. My father wheeled it into the living room where my mother and Layne the Favorite sat watching TV. He ran and jumped on his new bike. One of the pedals came off and clunked to the floor.

Mom: "Fred. What is wrong with you?"

Dad: "I think the fucking nut is missing."

I padded out to the living room, not a stitch of clothing on, and dropped the nut into my dad's hand.

Dad: "Thanks, Stace. Holy crap! Are you naked?"

Mom (dismissively): "He does that. Get back to bed, Buster."

Sunday night.

I was sent to bed at seven thirty. Layne the Favorite was riding his new bike in a circle around the part of our driveway inside the fence. The giant gate kept him from skittering down the long driveway into traffic and being flattened like a bug, after which all the goats in the land would be mine, as it says in the Old Testament. At eight o'clock the theme for *Sanford and Son* came on. I stripped naked and went out to the living room, where my mother sat alone on the couch with no popcorn.

Me: "I'll watch TV with you."

Mom: "Get to bed, Buster."

I went out to the back porch and sat on the top step, watching Layne the Favorite ride his new bike in a circle. A few loose parts that had fallen off twinkled in the dim remaining light of day.

Me: "Having fun?"

Layne the Favorite (defiantly): "Yes I am! Where are your clothes?"

Me: "Wouldn't it be more fun to ride bikes with someone?"

Layne the Favorite pondered as he circled, his tires crunching on nuts and bolts. The brakes locked and the bike stopped short. He toppled over and sprawled onto the driveway. He stood up, kicked the bike, and stormed past me into the house. I followed. It was getting too cold to be outside naked.

Mom: "Layner, what happened?"

Layne the Favorite: "My bike broke. Daddy messed it up."

Mom: "That son of a bitch. I'll pay the store to do it right. It's worth it for you to be safe."

Layne the Favorite: "I want a new one."

He jerked his head at me. "He can have my old one. Then we can ride bikes together."

Me: "Holy crap!" Layne the Favorite rarely suggested we do anything together. Nor did I ever get any of his old possessions, no matter how much he hated them.

Mom: "Get to bed, you."

***

LAYNE THE FAVORITE got a new bike two days after he got a new bike. This one was assembled at the store for seven dollars. His old bike was wheeled into a corner by the back stairs. Even though I was due to inherit it, I was not allowed to touch it until his new bike had been delivered.

Monday night, he went outside to ride after dinner. Finally allowed to lay hands on my new bike, I tried to ride it, but whatever calamity had struck it the night before made it unusable. I went to my mother with the problem.

Me: "My bike doesn't work."

Mom: "Isn't it time for bed?"

Me: "It's six o'clock."

Mom (holding up her arm): "Do you see it, Sssstace? Do you see my watch?"

Me: "How do I get my bike fixed?"

Mom: "Maybe you should call your father. I'm sure he'll come running over. Son of a bitch."

I went back outside. My next door neighbor, Jimmy the Third (father of my friend Jimmy the Fourth) had seen me struggling with the bike from his third floor window, where he spent a lot of time watching the neighborhood, and came over to have a look. He had the bike upside down and was tinkering with the chain.

Jimmy the Third: "So it just stopped."

Layne the Favorite (riding his new bike in a circle): "Stopped short. Mom says I could have been badly hurt."

Jimmy the Third: "Who put it together?"

Layne the Favorite: "My dad. That son of a bitch."

Jimmy the Third nodded. He did some more work on the chain, flipped the bike over, looked at me, and patted the seat.

Jimmy the Third: "Give it a try, sport."

I hopped on the bike and was able to pedal a few feet without trouble.

Jimmy the Third: "Have fun. Try to keep your clothes on, will ya?"

My seven thirty bedtime was suspended starting that day: Layne the Favorite needed someone to ride bikes with. A few days later we were in the driveway close to the big gate. He was having a particularly fun time racing toward me at top speed and swerving at the last minute. I didn't care. I was outside in the dark, fully-clothed, riding a bike.

Layne the Favorite charged at me on his bike, grinning ferally. I pedaled faster, as I usually did to get out of his way. The handlebars fell off, clunked to the ground, and I had nothing to hold on to. He was so surprised that he forgot to swerve and crashed into my bike, sending me face first into the gate. Something sliced my eyebrow open and I fell to the ground, bleeding, my bike and his bike on top of me. Layne the Favorite bolted silently to the back door and inside the house.

I don't know how long I lay there, but I looked up to see Jimmy the Third leaning over me. He had pulled the bikes off of me and was holding his shirt to my forehead.

Me: "I may have crashed my new bike."

Jimmy the Third picked me up and carried me inside. He put me down on the couch next to my mother and Layne the Favorite, who were watching *All in the Family*.

Mom: "What happened to him?"

Jimmy the Third: "He hit the fence with his head."

Mom: "If he'd been in bed on time, this wouldn't have happened."

Jimmy the Third: "It's only eight o'clock."

Mom (holding up her arm): "Look at this, Johnny! I got a watch!"

Jimmy the Third: "Your son's got a nasty cut. He's going to need stitches."

Mom: "For that? It's nothing. A scratch."

Jimmy the Third: "He's bleeding pretty badly."

Mom: "He needs to go to bed."

Jimmy the Third went to the phone on the wall and dialed. He spoke briefly, gave our address, and hung up.

Jimmy the Third: "Ambulance is on the way."

Mom: "No way, Jerry! He doesn't need a goddamned ambulance! Who's gonna pay for it? Not his stinkin' father, that son of a bitch!"

Sanford and Son came up on the TV, with its catchy theme. I started to take my pants off.

Jimmy the Third: "What is *wrong* with him?"

Mom (shrugging): "No idea, Jackie. I keep asking him that and never get an answer."

Jimmy the Third: "My name's Jimmy." The men of his line had been named Jimmy for a hundred years.

Mom: "That's what I said."

I got five stitches and Jimmy the Third snuck over the next day, took my bike home, and completely rebuilt it. As a success, I would have to say it was a mixed bag:

1. New bike.
2. A dispensation on my seven thirty bedtime, although Layne the Favorite started going in around eight anyway to watch TV with his mother, at which time I got sent to bed.
3. Five stitches and a scar for life.

I knew how Philip II of Spain felt, having a post-Armada tantrum in the palace in Madrid.

Philip II of Spain: "I sent a hundred and thirty ships! What the hell happened?"

I felt the pain of the ancient Hannibal, sulking in his tent, tears leaking from his one good eye.

Hannibal: "I brought elephants, for Jupiter's sake. *Elephants*."

My days took on a grindingly similar routine: ride bikes with Layne the Favorite until around eight. My mother would stick her head out the back window and call for him and we would both have to go inside. She had stopped telling me to get to bed - I just knew.

Eight pm. *Sanford and Son* came on TV. I went to bed, but I wasn't going to stay there.

And I was buck-ass naked.

4

MY MOTHER THE DOCTOR

I HAD BEEN spitting blood with an Old Faithful-like regularity all day, but it took a man with white shoes to notice.

Larry the Straight Hairdresser: "Carol! Your kid's spitting blood!"

Mom: "What are you talking about? I'm looking right at him. He's fine."

Larry the Straight Hairdresser: "The other kid. Number Two."

My mother was doing someone's hair in another part of the shop. While she was building up her own clientele for her new hair salon, she worked Saturdays for Larry the Straight Hairdresser. It was his busiest day of the week and my mother was the only one he could trust not to poach his customers.

He told me that my mother was an expert at handling his bitchiest clients. They were all women older than seventy, widowed, crotchety, and cheap. My mother called them the *Alter Kockers*, which was Yiddish for *old operator*. She talked to them in low, commiserating tones about their dead husbands, the rotten schmuck who lived next door, or the goddamned kosher butcher who was producing sub-par chopped liver.

Larry the Straight Hairdresser: "Carol. Althea gave you a tip?"

Mom: "Of course she did. I told her, I do her hair on a Saturday, she's not walking out of here without tipping me. It's like stealing!"

Larry the Straight Hairdresser: "Who's the son of a bitch she keeps talking about?"

Mom: "Her husband. Luther."

Larry the Straight Hairdresser: "You mean Louis?"

Mom: "That's what I said. Lawton."

Larry the Straight Hairdresser: "They were married forty years!"

Mom: "They're all sons of bitches, Larry."

Indeed they were. After a few Saturdays of my mother working at Larry the Straight Hairdresser's salon, all the Alter Kockers were calling their departed husbands "that son of a bitch" and tipping my mother huge wads of the dead fellow's cash.

Layne the Favorite was with her, busy playing with his Matchbox cars that no one, especially me, was allowed to touch. They had their own carrying case and a list of rules longer than the Bill of Rights.

"No one is allowed to touch these," he would remind our mother. That was rule number one. It was part of the packing-up ritual of the Matchbox cars - they went in their carrying case, each one carefully placed in the same order in the little parking spots in the box. When every one of them was accounted for, he would tell her that no one was allowed to touch them.

Me: "He means me."

Mom: "SSSSSStace. He does not. Your brother shares everything with you."

Not true then or ever. Overcoming my mother's certainty was impossible, so I tried the Socratic method:

Me: "You mean me, don't you, Layne?"

Layne the Favorite: "I mean anyone."

Me: "Like the mailman?"

Layne the Favorite: "Why would he want to play with my cars?"

Me: "The meter reader from the gas company?"

Layne the Favorite: "How would he even know I have them?"

Me: "Aunt Hchachel? Uncle Ruben?"

Mom: "Uncle Ruben lives in upstate New York. And Aunt Hchachel is ninety-two years old, SSSSStace. She's off her rocker."

That diagnosis, by the way, was from Dr. Mom. 'Dementia' was a weird, goyisher word. You could be "off your rocker", "cracked", or "meshuga." Never demented.

Me: "I thought she was cracked."

Mom: "She is. You think she's gonna play with Matchbox cars?"

Me: "It sounds just meshuga enough."

Mom: "What is *wrong* with you?"

Larry the Straight Hairdresser: "For one thing, he's spitting blood. From his mouth."

Me: "Layne. How about the serial killer who lives in the apartment upstairs?"

Mom: "He's not a serial killer. I keep telling you."

Me: "Would he tell you if he was?"

Mom: "Wouldn't we be his first targets?"

That actually made sense.

Me: "Mr. Vesley from the auto parts store?"

Layne the Favorite: "He has real cars to play with."

Wow. Everyone in my family was making sense that day. Perhaps I had fallen off *my* rocker. Actually, I had fallen off the roof of Mr. Vesley's auto parts store next door, hence the spitting blood and the failure of my Socratic method. The only other trick Socrates had had up his sleeve was to drink poison, walk around until his legs felt numb, then lay down and die. I figured I'd stick with asking questions.

Me: "How about Larry the Straight Hairdresser?"

Larry the Straight Hairdresser: "Don't knock it, kid. I get to hang out with women all day long."

Pppppppt - I spit blood on both of his shiny white shoes. Even straight guys needed their shoes to match. Especially ones who wore flamboyantly striped shirts unbuttoned halfway down to reveal gold medallions and a thicket of chest hair.

Larry the Straight Hairdresser gestured elegantly at his bloody shoes. "I told you so, Carol."

Mom: "SSSSSSSStace. You're spitting blood! Why are you doing that?"

Me: "Jimmy and I jumped off of Vesley's roof."

Mom: "No you didn't."

***

JIMMY THE FOURTH was the youngest child of our next door neighbor, Jimmy the Third. I liked the fact that all the men in the family were named Jimmy, as if they were royalty, and not girls. Jimmy the Fourth organized nightly baseball games in our back yard, which my mother had paved over to make a parking lot for her new beauty salon. I stayed out of the games, but Layne the Favorite was always involved.

Jimmy the Fourth, among his myriad of talents, was a top-notch pitcher, which was the position Layne the Favorite coveted. He never asked to pitch, but complained about Jimmy's monopoly of the mound all summer long, until my mother had to go have words with Jimmy one night after dinner.

Mom: "Johnny —"

Jimmy the Fourth: "Jimmy."

Mom: "That's what I said. Listen. My son wants a turn pitching the ball."

Jimmy the Fourth: "I had no idea."

Mom: "How could you have no idea? Josh, my son has a real talent. Don't tell me you couldn't tell. He's a natural!"

Jimmy the Fourth: "Okay then, Mrs. Roberts. He can pitch at our next game."

Mom: "You know, Joey, I never liked your parents much. But you seem all right. You're a good boy."

At the next game that formed in my back yard, Jimmy the Fourth tossed the ball to Layne the Favorite and switched places with him, ending up at shortstop. Layne the Favorite, without a word, went to the mound, did a dramatic, leg in the air windup like someone had attached electrodes to his ass, and flung the ball over the batter's head on to Vesley's roof.

Jimmy the Fourth: "Try again." He tossed him another ball.

He did his epileptic windup again. Ball on roof. The supply of game balls was down to one.

Jimmy the Fourth: (tossing the ball to me): "Your turn."

The ball hit me square in the chest and bounced off. It rolled to Layne the Favorite, who picked it up and prepared his Windmill Gambit.

Jimmy the Fourth: "Hold on, Layne." The windmill stopped.

Layne the Favorite: "He can't play. He's too little."

Jimmy the Fourth: "Pitchers don't have to be big. They just need a good arm. He looks like he's got one."

I looked at my arm quizzically. Jimmy nodded at me.

I walked slowly to the wooden slat on the ground that passed for a pitcher's mound. I looked at Layne the Favorite and then Jimmy the Fourth.

Me: "It's the last ball. If it goes on the roof..."

Layne the Favorite: "Then you screwed it up for everyone. Game over. Forget it. I'm pitching."

Jimmy the Fourth: "Then we come back tomorrow. With more balls."

Layne the Favorite went back to shortstop and Jimmy the Fourth stayed at the mound. I waited, thinking he was going to give me some pointers, or a warning about the treacherous low roof. The batter, Kevin Fagin, who later that year got "runned over" by a car, yet lived to tell about it, waited in silence. There was a chalked-in box on the third rail of the wood fence that was the strike zone.

Jimmy the Fourth: "Pitch."

Me: "What?"

Jimmy the Fourth (quietly): "You're gonna have to pitch before Kevin wets himself." Kevin had a notoriously weak bladder and a loose sphincter. He was the only one of our group who had ever shat in the woods. As my mother would say, "Disgusting."

Me (even more quietly): "If I miss..."

Jimmy the Fourth: "You won't miss. I've been watching you practice."

I had spent hours - usually in the rain - pitching tennis balls against the fence. I picked early morning and inclement weather to practice in because all the neighborhood kids were inside. It never occurred to me that Jimmy the Fourth might have been watching from his window. If he thought I could do it, that was all I needed. Jimmy the Fourth was the neighborhood's rock solid truth teller. I never saw him lie, even to spare someone's feelings, like the time he took Kevin aside on one of our gallivanting trips far from home:

Jimmy the Fourth: "Kevin. You wet yourself."

Kevin the Weak Bladdered: "No I didn't. I fell in a puddle."

Jimmy the Fourth: "Okay. Do you need to go home? We can go back now if you want."

Kevin the Weak Bladdered: "No big deal. Just a puddle. I'm fine."

Later that day, Kevin the Weak Bladdered shat himself as well. I never heard his explanation for that. I would like to say that I myself never used the *fell crotch first into a puddle* defense, but that would be a lie.

I stood on the mound and readied myself. Kevin held the bat. I could see him fidgeting; his bladder was working against him. He was one pitch away from a walk and a minute from calling a time out so he could sprint to a secluded tree.

I wound up and hurled the ball. It hit the fence slat just inside the strike zone.

Jimmy the Fourth: "That's strike one."

He stood with his arms folded. The ball rolled to him and he picked it up and tossed it to me. I threw again, and this time Kevin swung at it almost immediately. I wasn't in the strike zone that time, but Kevin missed the ball. Strike two.

Jimmy the Fourth (putting the ball in my hand): "One more."

I threw again. Kevin didn't move at all. The ball sailed under his bat, smacked the fence in the center of the strike zone, and rolled slowly back to the mound. Kevin dropped the bat and sprinted for his favorite pee tree.

Jimmy the Fourth: "I think we found our new pitcher."

Layne the Favorite stomped off toward the house. I could hear my mother's voice as soon as he opened the door: "Layner, what happened?"

***

Jimmy the Fourth (standing behind me): "You want to get up on the roof."

Me: "Nuh uh."

Jimmy the Fourth: "What's your plan?"

Me: "Plan? No plan. Nothing going on here."

Jimmy the Fourth: "What's your plan?"

Me: "Top of fence, foot on tree, climb up to roof."

Jimmy the Fourth: "That should work. How will you get down?"

Me: "Same way."

Jimmy the Fourth: "You'll end up in the rusty junk pile. Stuck like a bug."

Between Vesley's shop and my fence was a pile of discarded, rusty things like old tools, a water heater, and broken car parts.

We studied the problem for a few minutes in silence. Then Jimmy the Fourth had an idea:

Jimmy the Fourth: "The guy who lives upstairs from you put three mattresses out for the garbage. We could jump down from the roof."

Three things:

1. Mattresses from the serial killer upstairs? Stained with the tears of his hapless victims? Yuck.
2. He said "we." My solitary plan had now become a conspiracy.
3. Jump off the roof?

Jimmy the Fourth: "Why not just get a ladder?"

Of course I had thought about it. Jimmy the Fourth's dad was an electrician and came home every day in a truck that had extension ladders hung on the sides. Lay one of those bad boys against the side of the building and I'd be up and back without any trouble at all, and more importantly, no lockjaw or slow rusty death.

But asking for a ladder, even one from my mother, would elevate my project above the radar. I could build my own ladder out of plutonium rods and frayed clothesline and get a rabid pit bull to hold it steady for me and no one would notice or care. If I asked to borrow a ladder, I would be strapped to a chair in my Underroos, a single bare bulb overhead, deprived of food and water, kept awake against my will, and interrogated as to my nefarious purpose.

Me: "Anyone can get up on a roof with a *ladder*."

He grinned, and we went to get the mattresses.

The serial killer upstairs had thrown out three queen sized mattresses. That seemed weird to me. The apartment wasn't big enough for three queen sized beds.

Me: "What does he need with three mattresses?"

Jimmy the Fourth: "It's probably better for us to think about what we need with them. When we're done, they go back in the trash."

We stacked the mattresses close to my side of the fence, two in one pile and the third in front of it. That way, Jimmy the Fourth said, we wouldn't bounce off the stack of mattresses and land on the hard asphalt my backyard was paved with. Jimmy the Fourth climbed the wooden fence, up past the strike zone, to the top. He put one hand on the trunk of the cherry tree to steady himself, then reached up to the roof. He grabbed the roof at the edge, put one foot on a knot in the cherry tree, and alternately pulled with his arms and pushed with his foot, catapulting himself onto the flat roof.

He was gone from sight. After a moment, his head appeared at the roof line.

Jimmy the Fourth: "Easy. Come on up."

As I climbed to the top of the fence, I couldn't help looking down at the narrow alley of rusted metal - an old water heater, crumbling pipes, and cruel shards of brown metal waiting for me to land on. I stood on the top rail of the fence, feeling the weak, weathered wood bow beneath my feet. I steadied myself on the trunk of the cherry tree and looked up.

Jimmy the Fourth: "Push off with your feet as hard as you can. There's nowhere to go but up."

I hooked my fingers on as much of the roof as I could. The gritty shingles felt like moonscape or the surface of an alien planet. I put my right foot on the same tree knot Jimmy the Fourth had used, and pushed off with all my strength while pulling up as hard as I could. As I passed the level of the roof, my pull changed to a modified pushup and Jimmy the Fourth grabbed my shirt and hauled me up and over, onto the roof of Vesley's.

I was finally there. The roof stretched out before me, flat, gray, and gritty, with occasional islands where air conditioning units and exhaust vents broke up the landscape. All the stuff that had found their way up to the low roof was there: baseballs, tennis balls, bats, footballs, basketballs, caps with different team logos on them, old auto parts, clothes, shoes, and the scissors used back in 1958 to cut the ceremonial ribbon across the doors of the store on its opening day.

Jimmy the Fourth and I spent half an hour chucking all this stuff off the roof and on to the mattresses below. When it was cleared, we walked from end to end, looking out over a huge expanse of our neighborhood. Like any kid who slept in a basement next to a furnace, I entertained fantasies of living up there on the roof, maybe in a tent, peeing over the side into the desolate lot behind the store and using a ladder to come down when it was time for school.

We stood at the edge of the roof, looking at the mattresses.

Jimmy the Fourth: "Time to jump."

There was no weaseling out. I wanted to ask him to call out to his dad and have him bring us a ladder. I wanted to ask him to wait for someone to come outside and notice the two of us standing up on the roof. But that wasn't what you did with Jimmy the Fourth. When it was time to jump, you jumped.

Jimmy the Fourth: "I'll go first. I'll show you how to do it."

I just nodded. He stepped back a few paces, then walked to the edge again. He backed up once more, ran a few steps, and leaped into the air. My heart stopped.

He landed on the larger stack of mattresses, bent at the knees, and rolled onto the single one. He got to his feet gracefully and looked up at me.

Jimmy the Fourth: "Easy enough. Take a running start and jump for the mattresses."

I shook my head no.

Jimmy the Fourth: "You can do it."

It was all I needed. I took a few steps back and looked around one last time. If I was going to die after leaping, I wanted to remember what the world looked like from the roof of the auto parts store - my house, the street behind it, the metal processing plant, the twinkling of sunlight off the cars in Vesley's parking lot, the pile of accumulated lost items that we had liberated from captivity.

Jimmy the Fourth: "Don't hesitate. Be brave."

I ran a few steps and jumped.

It seemed like I was suspended in the air for several long minutes. I was as high as the trees. My feet hovered above the center of the highest stack of mattresses. I grinned as I landed, a huge bright smile that allowed my bent knees to easily find my front teeth. The impact was horrific. I heard a cracking sound, saw stars, peed my pants, and rolled onto the single mattress. I lay on my back on the serial killer's bedding.

Jimmy the Fourth: "You made it!"

Jimmy the Fourth: "You're bleeding."

Jimmy the Fourth: "You wet yourself."

Me (eyes closed): "Puddle."

Jimmy the Fourth: "Can you get up?"

He helped me to my feet. My head was reeling. I could taste iron in my mouth. I spat blood onto the mattress. Pppppppppt.

Jimmy the Fourth: "You go inside. I'll drag the mattresses to the street."

I staggered home and took a shower, spitting blood into the drain. My two front teeth felt numb when I probed them with my tongue. Numb was good, right? I explained it to Larry the Straight Hairdresser as he took me outside his salon to look at my teeth. He reached two of his soft, chemical-smelling fingers into my mouth and gently wiggled one of them.

Larry the Straight Hairdresser: "Your teeth are loose. What happened?"

Me: "Layne hit me. I played with one of his Matchbox cars."

Larry the Straight Hairdresser: "What really happened?"

Me: "Jumped off a roof."

Larry the Straight Hairdresser: "You're lucky to be alive. Let's go talk to your mother. She acts like she's been to medical school."

Mom: "Larry. He doesn't need to go to the dentist. His teeth are a little loose. That's all."

Larry the Straight Hairdresser: "He's still bleeding. He's probably been bleeding all day."

Me: "Pppppppppppt."

Mom: "SSSSSSSStace. Stop spitting blood on Larry's shoes!"

Larry the Straight Hairdresser: "Carol, if you don't take him to the dentist, I will."

***

I SAT IN the dentist chair while my mother looked around the room, reading notices tacked up on the wall. I should have paid more attention to what she was looking at.

Dentist: "Mrs. Roberts. His two front teeth are definitely loose." He looked at me.

Dentist: "What did you hit them with?"

Me: "My knees."

Dentist: "Okay, then. Nothing to worry about. I'll give him a shot of Novocaine straight into the gums to numb them up, then we'll pull them out. They're baby teeth, so the permanent ones should drop in soon enough."

Mom: "Novocaine? He can't have Novocaine!" She pointed at one of the notices she had been reading. "It says that you shouldn't have Novocaine if you have a heart condition."

Dentist: "Does he have a heart condition?"

Mom: "He's a preemie!"

Dentist: "What?"

Mom: "Premature! He was two months early! His lungs weren't cooked! I bet he has a heart condition!"

Dentist: "Has he been seen by a cardiologist?"

Mom (teeth gritted): "I don't need a stinkin' cardiologist to tell me about his heart. I was *there*. He's a preemie!"

Dentist: "Okay. We'll go without Novocaine."

For about ten seconds, I was relieved that I wasn't going to have to get a shot. I hated shots. It turns out I hated having my teeth pulled without Novocaine even more.

***

BACK AT LARRY the Straight Hairdresser's shop, I sat miserably in a chair with cotton stuffed up against the holes where my teeth had been. We always had good teeth in my family; it was why I still had baby teeth at age nine. In fact, I still have a baby tooth now. It's because I was a preemie. I'm sure of it.

My head was killing me. Larry the Straight Hairdresser could tell:

Larry the Straight Hairdresser: "Do you want an aspirin?"

I nodded.

Mom: "No way! Do you know what aspirin does to you? It shreds your intestinal lining!"

Me: "I'll rithk it."

Mom: "Absolutely not! He can't have any goddamned aspirin. He was a preemie! He's lucky to be alive! You're not going to shred his intestines!"

Larry the Straight Hairdresser shrugged. "At least now you've got your own song."

Me: "What?"

Larry the Straight Hairdresser: "All I want for Christmas is my two front teeth."

Mom: "We do NOT celebrate Christmas!"

Layne the Favorite, knowing we were leaving soon, packed up all his Matchbox cars. He looked at my mother.

Layne the Favorite: "No one touches these. No one."

Mom: "That's right, honey."

***

WE DROVE HOME in blissful silence. My head felt like it had been hit by a couple of high-speed knees.

Mom: "What is all that crap on the back porch?"

I roused myself from my toothless stupor and lifted my aching head so I could see. The back porch was covered with baseballs, footballs, tennis balls, bats, caps, and the opening day scissors from Vesley's ribbon cutting in 1958.

It hurt to smile.

5

SPIT BOWL

One Saturday morning in 1987, I couldn't swallow, but I didn't panic. I'd go downstairs, inform my mother of the problem, and she would whisk me away to a doctor and a pharmacy, and I'd be as good as new by nightfall.

Yeah, right.

Instead, I began the ancient healing ritual.

We Jews live by rituals – special cups on the Sabbath, wineglasses broken under our heels at weddings, flat crackers on Passover, eight candles at Hanukkah, and soul crushing guilt on Yom Kippur. For this occasion, I had a ritual.

The vestments: from the back of my closet, I got the robe I had inherited when Ted the Drug Dealer got arrested. It was the color of crusty dried blood, way too big for me, and the matching belt was long gone. In its place, the robe was secured with a length of blue and white rope. I had a pair of old boat shoes that I used as slippers. I added boxer shorts and a gray T-shirt that used to be white.

The relics: on the way downstairs I stopped in the kitchen to get an ugly, scratched, plastic bowl. I also grabbed a cup that didn't match with a lid and straw.

The sacrament: I filled the cup with tepid tap water, screwed down the lid, and jammed the straw in it.

The altar: I hauled my ailing carcass to the couch. I sat heavily, lined up the bowl and the cup, and clicked on the TV.

An hour later, my mother came downstairs and stared at me in my regalia with my collection of icons arranged in front of me.

Mom: "SSSSSSStace. What is *wrong* with you?"

I spat into the bowl.

Me: "Tonsillitis."

I had gotten tonsillitis at least once a year since the age of eleven. It started with painful fishhook swallowing, then fever, and ultimately, swelling of the throat. Three days in, I wouldn't be able to get down anything more substantial than tepid water. By the fourth day, I couldn't even swallow my own saliva. Hence the bowl, which needed to be emptied several times a day.

Mom: "Disgusting."

The summer before, my tonsillitis episode had lasted eight days. I lost twelve pounds. No doctor was called. No prescription was filled. My mother would not have it.

Me: "Well, here we are again, Ma. Tonsillitis."

Mom: "So what do you want me to do about it? Do you know what tonsils do? They're crap catchers! They catch crap!"

Me: "And then get inflamed and putrid."

Mom: "What then, smart guy? You want all those toxins running around your system? It'll kill your cells! You want dead cells? Your tonsils are saving you from toxins."

Me: "So let's reward them with a nice field trip to the doctor."

Mom: "Doctors shmocktors. I don't know what you think a doctor's gonna do for you."

Me: "Good news! In 1928, Alexander Fleming grew a substance from bread mold that, as it turned out —"

Mom: "I don't want to hear that bullcrap."

Me: "—killed a number of disease-causing bacteria. He named the substance penicillin."

Mom: "SSSSSStace. You don't ever listen to me. Penicillin interferes with your body's defenssssssses. You need to be able to fight off infection without any help."

Me: "How about some aspirin, then?"

Mom: "No way! I told you - it shreds your intestines! You were a preemie, Stace. Do you understand what I'm saying? A preemie!"

I was born two months earlier than my anticipated due date and weighed two and a quarter pounds. There are some skeptics who think my mother's pack a day cigarette habit was contributory, but I think we all know that's utter nonsense.

Me: "Chloraseptic?"

She shook her head and sniffed disdainfully.

Mom: "All that does is take away the pain."

Me: "Which is wrong."

Mom: "Damned right! You can't mask your symptoms with crap like that."

Me: "Why not? What good does it do to know what your symptoms are if there's NO TREATMENT?" That hurt my throat. My mother stood up and went into the kitchen. I spat into the bowl. Pppppppppppppppt.

Mom: "Disgusting."

* * *

Day Four.

I had kicked the slippers on to the floor. The robe was piled up on a corner of the couch. My shirt was dark with sweat. I kept dozing off, so everything I was watching on TV was jumbled. The car from Knight Rider crashed into the apartment that Jack shared with Chrissy and Janet. Mr. Roper was so furious he moved to Hawaii and solved crimes while living on Robin Masters' estate.

My friend Rob called on Day Five.

Rob: "Is Stacey there?"

Me: "It's me."

Rob: "You sound like an old man."

Me: "I've had tonsillitis for four days."

Rob: "The antibiotics must not be working."

Me: "No antibiotics."

Rob: "Are you fucking kidding me?"

Me: "My mom won't let me have any."

Rob: "My mom's got some pills left over from an ear infection she had a few months ago. I've got some other shit around here you can use. I'm on my way."

Me (croaking weakly): "Chloraseptic!"

Rob: "Got it. Be there in thirty."

***

IT WAS DARK when I woke up. At the time that I dozed off, I had left Magnum, PI in a very precarious situation, eating pie at Mel's Diner. Now, as my body shook from chills, George Jefferson sat in Archie Bunker's chair, on the Fonz's lap.

I reached out a weak, clammy hand and dragged my robe over, covering myself with it. On the coffee table in front of me was only my half-filled phlegm bowl and an empty cup of water. I swallowed hard and closed my eyes against the pain. Tears ran down my cheeks.

Me (rasping): "Where is it? Rob, you bastard."

Mom: "What are you talking about?"

Me: "Rob was supposed to bring me some stuff."

Mom: "What kind of stuff? What for?"

Me: "Ummmm...school. School stuff."

Mom: "It's summer."

Me: "The reading list. Hemingway's gonna be big this year."

My mother came over and looked down at me, barefoot, cowering under my robe, my hair drenched in sweat. Her contempt was palpable.

Mom: "SSSSStace. Do you know what a *dreykop* is?"

Me: "Yiddish for something you don't like."

Mom: "A bullshit artist."

Me: "I always wondered, where do they get their art supplies?"

Mom: "You're also a smartass. Too smart for your own good. Why can't you be more like your brother?"

Me: "Because I want to grow up and leave home one day. Maybe tomorrow."

Mom: "Your little friend was here, smarty pants. You were sleeping. He gave me the little care package he brought for you."

Me: "Son of a bitch."

Mom: "That reminds me. Call your father. Anyway. Ralph gave me the *reading list*."

Me: "Rob, Mom. His name is Rob."

Mom: "That's what I said. I dumped all that crap out. Those pills? The facochten amoxicillin? Flushed. I poured that Chloraseptic stuff down the drain too. You don't need that crap. I told you. There was some kind of soup in there his mother made. It's got noodles in it. I saved it for you."

Me: "Noodles? Are you kidding me? I can't swallow anything bigger than a hydrogen atom!"

Mom: "Then I'm throwing that out, too. Probably not kosher anyway. Where's his mother from? Somalia?"

Me: "The Dominican Republic."

Mom: "That's what I said. Anyway, I'm pitching it."

I changed the channel. The A-Team blew up the boarding school Mrs. Garrett ran. I felt bad for Tootie. When I woke up, it was morning, and I had a new plan.

Layne the Favorite: "You look terrible, little brother."

Me: "I was a preemie. Very sad. Anyway, Mom said she wanted you to go to the store and get me some Chloraseptic."

Layne the Favorite (chuckling): "No way! Listen. What do you need that crap for?"

Me: "It stops the pain."

Layne the Favorite: "Listen. The pain can't be that bad. You're a wimp."

When Layne the Favorite was six years old, he got tonsillitis for about four and a half minutes before my mother rushed him to the hospital to get them taken out. The party she threw for him when he came home was legendary. There was even cake. Cake!

He went on his way. I got up and emptied my spit bowl and left it in the sink. I put my boat shoes on, cinched my robe shut, and staggered upstairs.

Layne the Favorite had an honest to God piggy bank, heavy with coins that he had painstakingly saved for years. I raised it over my head and smashed it to bits on the floor. Coins flew everywhere like shrapnel. I sank to my knees and spent fifteen painful minutes scooping coins into the pockets of my robe, resting my feverish head against the bed.

Jingling, I left the house, concentrating on putting one foot in front of the other, wondering what that incessant wind chime noise was. It paused every time I stopped walking. Maybe it was the harsh, metallic sound my tonsils made while they ground my throat to shreds.

There was a Publix grocery store across the street from the complex we lived in. I got a lot of funny looks from the people I passed. My hair was stiff and unwashed, face pale, eyes wild and red. I jangled with stolen coins, spitting every time I needed to swallow, wearing a drug dealer's bathrobe two sizes too big for me.

The air conditioning in the store felt wonderfully cold on my fevered body. I shuffled to the pharmacy aisle and found the biggest bottle of Chloroseptic they had. I ripped the plastic off of it, flung the protective cap down the aisle, and sprayed my swollen, festering tonsils twenty times. I hung my head and swallowed without any pain. My own spit tasted like dinner in a five-star restaurant.

I plunked the bottle down on the checkout line belt. The cashier, a fifty-something woman with hair dyed violently red like my mother's, did a double-take at the sight of me.

Cashier: "Any coupons today?"

I stared at her. She shrugged.

Cashier: "That'll be eleven fifty."

I reached in my pocket and started handing her coins. She took them in her cupped hands and counted them out into small piles. The people in line behind me, already intrigued by my decrepit appearance, watched as I emptied my robe. She finished counting and looked at me expectantly.

Cashier: "You've only got eight fifteen here."

I hung my head.

Me: "Then call the cops, cause I'm taking this with me. I live across the street. I'll leave the door open for them."

Cashier (gently): "What's wrong with you?"

Me: "Tonsillitis. Day five."

Burly Black Man (in line behind me): "Day five? Who the hell has tonsillitis for five days? Go to the damn doctor, boy, and quit shoplifting."

Me (indignantly): "I'm not shoplifting. I just didn't steal enough money to pay for the whole thing."

The Burly Black Man folded his arms. The orange-haired cashier was reaching for something under the cash register. Probably the panic button. The jig was indeed up.

Me: "Is there a place I can sit down while I wait for the cops? I don't think my legs will hold me up anymore."

The cashier pulled out the thing she had been reaching for. It was her purse. She took out four dollar bills, opened the drawer, and put them in. She expertly made change for herself and handed me the receipt.

Cashier: "Have a good day."

Burly Black Man: "Go to the damn doctor."

I staggered home and collapsed on the couch, stuffing the Chloroseptic bottle between the cushions underneath me. I grinned, feeling its pointy lump poking the back of my thigh as I settled into my first pain-free sleep in nearly a week.

Layne the Favorite swore up and down that there had been over fifty dollars in that pig.

Me: "Bullshit. Except for what rolled under the bed, there was about eight bucks in there."

Mom: "The money doesn't matter, SSSSSSStace. That was his and you took it. Do you know how hurt he is?"

Me: "Anything like, say, razor blades in one's throat?"

TRAILER TRASH, WITH A GIRL'S NAME

Mom (staring at me blankly): "I don't know what you're talking about. But you listen to me, Buster. You're gonna pay him back every cent of that money."

Me: "I thought the money didn't matter. How about a sincere apology? Perhaps a hug?"

Mom: "You pay him back. Every cent."

That was the most expensive bottle of Chloraseptic anyone ever bought. It cost me fifty-seven dollars, but it was worth it. Whatever magic elixir it contained, it kept me from having my annual bout with tonsillitis until my second year of college.

Even though I had been on a roll, when I moved away for college, I still packed my robe, T-shirt, boxer shorts, and boat shoes. Plus what remained of the bottle of Chloraseptic. The essence of any religion is faith and ritual. Just ask that goyisher Pope.

✳✳✳

OCTOBER, 1989. IT hurt to swallow when I woke up. I knew just what to do.

My friend Mark, my roommate, came home from class one day to find me wearing the maroon robe and boat shoes, sprawled on the couch, with a half filled spit bowl on the table in front of me. In its new place of honor, my latest holy relic, was the half full bottle of Chloraseptic, like the pinky finger of Judah the Maccabee. I was flipping channels between MTV and VH1.

Mark: "What is *wrong* with you?"

Me (shrugging eloquently): "Tonsillitis."

Mark: "Go to the doctor."

Me: "Blasphemy. Can't knock down my body's natural defenses. Three more days on the couch and I'll be good as new."

Mark: "What's the bowl for?"

I told him.

Mark: "Get dressed and get in the car. I'm taking you to the clinic on campus."

Me: "It's perfectly fine. I've got a system."

Mark (nodding): "If you're not in the car in five minutes, I'm going to pick you up, robe and all, dump your ass in the trunk, and drive you to campus."

I emptied my spit bowl and was in the car in three minutes flat.

The doctor at the clinic was amazed.

Doc: "You have the worst case of tonsillitis I've ever seen."

Me: "My mother would be so proud. Let's take these bad boys out!"

Doc (shaking her head): "We don't take tonsils out any more. Apparently they serve a real purpose."

Me: "Just this once? I won't tell the AMA. Or my mom."

Doc: "No can do." She prepped a long needle and syringe.

Me: "Let's be reasonable. There's no need for a shot of any kind."

The doctor grinned, opened a bottle, and handed me a pill and a paper cup of water.

Doc: "Fine. Take this."

The pill was the size of a fat baby's fist. I stared at it, swallowed nervously, and my whole face crinkled with pain.

Me: "How about we smash it to a fine powder and dissolve it in some kind of liquid instead? Fun, right? Science-like! Very doctory."

Doc: "Did that already. It's in the syringe."

Me: "What happened to 'first, do no harm?'"

Doc: "Outdated. That oath is two thousand years old or something."

Me: "Did you go to medical school at this college?"

Doc: "Bend over."

I walked away from that meeting with a sore posterior and a bottle of pills. By the end of that day, I could swallow them. At the end of the next, I was cured.

I hid the nearly-full container of antibiotics in the pocket of my maroon robe. The other pocket held the half-full bottle of Chloraseptic.

Mark: "So you took all of the antibiotics, right?"

Me (with dewy eyed innocence): "Whatever do you mean?"

Mark: "You have to take them all."

Me: "But I'm cured! Huzzah!"

Mark: "Take all the pills, or I'm gonna —"

I ran for my robe before he finished talking.

6

WHEN IT'S YOUR TIME TO GO

WE WERE ALL doomed, and my mother knew it for sure.

"When it's your time to go, it's your time to go," she would say. The first time I heard it from her was around 1980, when we watched the movie *Meteor*, which was about the certain destruction of the entire planet. It had Sean Connery in it. He and his team worked around the clock to find ways to divert a meteor the size of Texas that was mere days away from pulverizing our cute little civilization. Mom just shook her head while she watched.

Mom: "No point. When it's your time to go, it's your time to go."

She repeated this over and over. I was nine, and not nearly ready to go.

Me: "But they've got missiles! They can blow that meteor to smithereens! Earth is saved! Huzzah!"

Mom (teeth clenched, jaw grinding): "Sssssstace. When it's your time to go, it's your time to go."

Me: "So they should just give up? Wait to get ka-blammed by the meteor?"

Mom: "I don't know what to tell ya. Let them try if they want. People should feel good about themselves."

Me: "But it won't matter."

Mom: "Not one little bit."

Me: "Okay."

In the movie, Earth was saved. I tried not to be smug.

Me: "Huzzah!"

Mom: "Movies aren't real."

She went to do the dishes.

***

EVEN AT AGE nine, I could see a problem. The woman whose job it was to keep me alive had taken up a blatant fatalism that I feared would not work out well for me:

1. I start to choke on a chicken bone from her unspeakable soup. She watches impassively as I gasp for air, pound my chest, turn blue, and sink under the table.
2. She retrieves the newspaper from our steep driveway without a second look as I point my skateboard into heavy traffic.
3. She glances up wordlessly as I prepare to leap from the roof of the auto parts store next door, aiming for a stack of mattresses inexpertly placed on the ground where I hoped to land.

4. Desperate for something edible, I try to start a fire in our hibachi grill with a box of coal I found in the basement, and the gasoline for the lawnmower. She looks out the window at me, kneeling in front of drenched coal, striking match after match, then turns away.

5. Our motor home loses its brakes on the hill overlooking Hoover Dam. She shrugs as we careen uncontrollably toward the lake, the dam, and its killer submerged turbines.

✳ ✳ ✳

THERE WAS NO hope of getting a straight answer out of my mother, so I went to her sister, Aunt Sissy. She was surprisingly down to earth, and to this day remains the only person I could really count on to explain my family to me.

Me: "My mom says that when it's your time to go, it's your time to go. Why?"

Aunt Sissy: "Because it is."

Me: "You have got to be kidding me. You too?"

Her black eyes were impish.

Aunt Sissy: "Has anyone ever gone *after* their time to go? Has anyone ever gone *before* their time to go?"

Swell. A logic argument. As if my mother was using a line of reasoning that was exquisitely Spock-like. Spockian. Spock-esque?

Me: "I'm not buying it. She made it sound as if there's no hope. No way to save yourself when death comes rolling your way."

She let me off the hook, and explained.

The women in my family on my mother's side all lived into their late nineties. Some stellar exceptions, like crazy Aunt Rose or Aunt Hchachel, made it to one hundred and beyond, freewheeling, demented, incontinent, uncomprehending, but alive. The men, by contrast, died young from stupid accidents.

The quick summary: Women in my family could say "when it's your time to go, it's your time to go" with Buddha's serenity, knowing that their time could be as long as a century. It was cop-out fatalism.

It's also what the women said when the men in my family invariably killed themselves off by some of the following means:

1. Crushed by a tractor when mowing the lawn. Grandpa, aged 55.
2. Falling off a grain elevator. Uncle Hymen, aged 46.
3. Playing golf in a thunderstorm. Uncle Louis, aged 57.
4. Not putting his glasses on before taking his pills and dying from the wrong combination. Cousin Shlomo, aged 43.
5. Electrocuted while trying to steal his neighbor's cable. Cousin Stuart, aged 51.

My mother delivered the bad news like this:

Mom: "Remember your Uncle Louis?"

Me: "No."

Mom: "SSSSSSSSSSSSSSStace. Of course you do. Uncle Louis. Aunt Hchachel's husband. His daughter is the zaftig blonde. Stella. Sheila. Stephanie. Whatever. Stace! Come on. Louis!"

That was way too many shrill names shouted at once.

Me: "No idea. Did I ever meet him?"

Mom: "No. They lived in upstate New York."

Me: "So why would I remember him?"

Mom: "Stace. He's your uncle!"

Me: "So what about him?"

She flapped her hand.

Mom: "Oh, he's dead."

Me: "I miss him already."

Mom: "You're just like your father. Why you gotta be such a smartass?"

Me: "Because I'm just like my father?"

Mom: "That's what I said. Why don't you ever listen to me?"

Me: "So. Uncle Louis died."

Mom: "Yes. That schmuck. He was playing golf with his buddies, the goyim, in a thunderstorm. Lightning hit the tree he was under and a branch got knocked off and hit him on the head."

How many rules did that violate?

1. Playing golf.
2. Hanging out with goyim.
3. Taking refuge under a tree in a thunderstorm.
4. Failing to look up at the loud cracking sound of the branch separating from the trunk of the tree.

Me: "So wasn't it a little dumb of him to be out golfing in a thunderstorm?"

Mom: "When it's your time to go, it's your time to go."

Me: "Ah."

Since all parenting, in part, is the distillation of lessons from above, here's what I learned:

1. Hire others to cut your grass.
2. Get your grain in its fully processed form.
3. No golf. Also, avoid non-Jews, thunderstorms, and trees.
4. Read your prescription bottles and instructions carefully.
5. Pay for cable.

Words to live by. For a hundred years. My plan: demented, free-wheeling, uncomprehending, incontinent longevity.

I'm not leaving the house again.

7

TED THE DRUG DEALER

My MOTHER MARRIED Ted the Drug Dealer in the summer of 1980, back when he was just Ted the Lightbulb Salesman. He won her over by knocking down some fence posts with his Cadillac.

We lived in a three story house during the Carter Administration. The house had a top floor apartment that I have never seen, even to this day. There was always a tenant up there. He was only ever referenced when my mother said things like "I'm going upstairs to get the rent from The Schmuck." He was a musician, or a painter, or a serial killer. He must not have been very good at any of these things – there were no hit rock bands or famous impressionist painters from Garwood, New Jersey. No unexplained murders, either.

After my father left, my mother went into business for herself as a hairdresser, which meant turning the first floor of the house into a beauty salon. We moved into the basement where a few years before, my Uncle George the Bastard had put in a kitchen and carpeted the two little rooms. The bigger one had a fold out couch where my mother stayed. My brother and I slept on another fold out couch in the smaller room, around the corner from the furnace. The pilot light and burners provided something of a night light. It was like sleeping near a campfire that gave off no heat. In the midst of the Cold War, I imagined we were living in an underground bunker after some apocalyptic nuclear nightmare.

Starting up her own business also meant she would need parking, so the back yard had to be paved over. Up until then we had had an above ground pool, grass, and a swing set. The pool was for Layne the Favorite. I think my mother believed that he would become a champion swimmer one day, as long as the Olympics came up with an event for swimmers who just went around and around at top speed in small circles. He could win the gold in the 400-meter Whirlpool. It was easy to imagine his dizzy-eyed, nauseated picture on a box of Wheaties.

The pool had to be taken down. The day it happened, there was a crowd of people assembled to assist:

1. My father, the Son of a Bitch.
2. Bernie the Disco Prince, a lanky fellow my mom was dating.
3. The UPS driver.
4. Bertha Levine - my mother's arch-nemesis from high school.
5. Bill, a twenty-something stoner she had hit with her car the year before.

She could get *anyone* to help her. It was like a superpower. In person, you had no chance at all. Her jaw would clench, and she would stare at you with her huge brown eyes and grimly say, "Fred. I need the pool taken down. For my businesssssssssssssssss."

This worked on my father because he didn't want to have to pay more than the $40 a month he was paying in child support. He had been married three times before and had other ex-wives and children to finance.

I think Bill the Stoner was there to have her sign lawsuit papers from when she had run him over with her car. The UPS driver was just trying to deliver a package, and that may have been the day that Bertha Levine finally worked up the nerve to translate all her high school pain and rage into a murder attempt on the architect of her misery. We all knew why Bernie the Disco Prince was there.

They all got the same treatment. "How do you expect me to sign for that package when I can't get that goddamned pool taken down? It's for my businesssssssss." Or "Bill, put those papers over there and help me get the pool taken down. Without my businessssss I haven't got a pot to piss in. You wanna get money out of me in the lawsuit? Then help me out. You can't get blood from a stone!"

Or poor Bertha Levine. "You brought a knife? Are you kidding me? What good is a knife gonna be? You can't dismantle a pool with a knife. Here, give me that and take this screwdriver instead. I always said, Bertha, back in high school, I told you, you weren't too bright. Not a lot of smarts up there in that empty head of yours. Too ugly to land a husband and dumb as a bag of matzo balls. Go outside. The kids will show you what to do."

I ended up working next to Bertha. She was red-faced, sweating, hair stringy, teeth gritted, hissing, "I hate her SO much!" over and over as she took the screws out of the side of the pool. The UPS man asked if I would sign for the package because he had to get on with his route. My father hung out near the fence posts that hadn't been taken down yet, chain smoking and glaring at Bernie the Disco Prince, who was preoccupied with the fact that the pool was still full of water.

Bernie the Disco Prince (every time he saw my mother): "Carol. There's still water in the pool."

She put her hands on her hips and stared at him.

Mom: "It'll be fine, Bernie. Don't worry about it."

Dad (muttering through a thick blue haze of cigarette smoke): "Idiot."

Me: "Um, Mom. I think the water's going to be a problem."

Bernie the Disco Prince shot me a grateful look. He had been dating her for three months and still hadn't figured out Layne was the favorite. Me being on his side was like the tiny nation of Lichtenstein jumping into World War II. Zero effect. I think Bertha Levine, who had only been there for two hours, knew Layne was the favorite. Maybe her backup plan was to kidnap him and not give him back until my mother admitted that Bertha was pretty AND smart. Bernie was a moron. I should have got him and Bertha together. If only there had been more time.

That was when Ted the Lightbulb Salesman arrived, driving his big, dark blue Cadillac. It turned like a giant hovercraft into our driveway and moseyed up the hill. He stopped at the wooden gate that blocked the driveway from the backyard. I couldn't wait for that gate to come down. My brother had rammed me with his bike when I was six and I hit it with my face. I needed five stitches in my eyebrow (I still have the scar). It was my only ambulance ride, and the only reason I went to the hospital was because a neighbor saw it happen and called 911. Otherwise my mother would have just put a band aid on it.

Ted got out of the Cadillac, wearing a traditional dark suit. He sold lightbulbs, which was the shorthand I used. Actually, he sold light fixtures and long fluorescent tube bulbs to big businesses, like chain grocery stores and manufacturing facilities. He had been across the street from our house, selling light bulbs to the metal processing plant, when he spied my mother in the yard and came over. After finding out she was starting her own businessssss, he was quick to offer to supply her with all the lighting she would need. All our home-type lighting had to come out and be replaced with something more appropriate, and he was just the guy to hook her up.

He stopped at the fence and gazed at her.

Ted the Lightbulb Salesman: "I've got those sample fixtures in the trunk if you want to take a look."

My father's eyes narrowed, and he started sniffing the air like an angry squirrel.

Mom: "Ted, I don't have time for that. I got all these people out here and they can't manage to get the goddamned pool down."

Bernie the Disco Prince: "It's still full of water."

She turned on him.

Mom: "What is *wrong* with you?"

My father snickered.

Ted looked at the pool for a minute, then went to the trunk of the Cadillac, opened it, and came back with a heavy sledgehammer in one hand. He walked over to the section of pool Bertha and I were working on. I backed away in a big hurry.

Me: "Bertha. We should get out of the way."

Bertha (snarling): "I hate you too. Demon spawn."

Ted whacked the flat side of the pool once with the sledgehammer and the whole wall collapsed like a burst balloon. A flood of water whooshed out, taking Bertha's legs out from under her and washing her most of the way down the hill, howling bubbly profanity the whole way. She ended up in the parking lot of the auto parts store that was next to our house, soaking wet, muddy, and madder than ever.

I tried to warn her. Maybe mom was right about her all along.

Bertha got to her feet, shook her fists at the sky, and screamed, her wet, dirty hair in her face, clothes soaked, and missing one shoe. She stomped to her car and squealed away in a cloud of exhaust. She never came back for her knife or her shoe. I'd like to think Bernie the Disco Prince retrieved it and brought it to her, like Prince Charming with the glass slipper, and the two of them lived happily ever after.

My mother grinned.

Mom: "There you go, Bernie. Goddamned thing's empty, so take it apart."

He did. It was easy work after that. It was also Bernie the Disco Prince's last day on our merry crew of day laborers.

Mom (looking back at Ted): "Can you do something about those fence posts?"

He looked at them, six square wooden posts standing in a line where our fence had once been. The fence had come down easy enough, but no one had been able to get the posts out of the ground. This was the 1979 equivalent of King Arthur pulling the sword from the stone.

Ted got back in the Cadillac without a word and backed out of the driveway. My father chortled.

Dad: "Another winner, there, Carol."

Mom: "Son of a bitch."

He shrugged and kept smoking.

I saw the Cadillac pull into the driveway of the place next door and slowly creep up to the first fence post. He put the bumper of the big car up against it and accelerated slowly and relentlessly until it popped out of the ground. He backed up and went for the next one.

My father flicked his cigarette into the wet remains of the pool.

Dad: "Pool's down. You kids have fun."

He headed for his car.

Mom: "Lotta help you are, Fred. This is for your kidsssssssssssssssss!"

Ted knocked all the posts down and for good measure, took out the gate I was so mad at.

So I was all right with Ted, up until the day he found a used Winnebago for sale, and suggested we all move into it. For five years.

8

FEAR IN A HANDFUL OF DUST

I ALWAYS THOUGHT my mother should co-author a cookbook. With Satan. It could be used in the prison kitchens of despotic third world countries. Here are some of her classic recipes:

Roast chicken - find a bird that died hard. Coat liberally in paprika. Fling into oven. Turn oven up to iron-ore smelter temperature. Serve dessicated, dusty, desert-dry fowl. Insist that everyone eating it loves your roast chicken.

Bone soup - Beef bone, stock pot full of water. Boil. Add rice. The result is a hellish tapioca. If your children gag while trying to choke it down, remind them that children somewhere in the world are starving, and by the way, you always loved my bone soup!

Macaroni and cheese - open blue box. Boil pasta and drain. Open dust packet. Pour on macaroni. Stir. Crunch away.

I had never had macaroni and cheese anywhere else - not at a friend's house or a restaurant. Like gravy, I suspect that's another non-Hebrew tradition, maybe because it goes so exquisitely well with ham. You know the kind I mean - thick elbow noodles, creamy cheese, bread crumbs, baked. Bottom line - I was in the dark about proper macaroni and cheese preparation. Ours was the gritty, kosher version, designed to remind us of so many years spent trudging through sand. Like the Passover vegetables dipped in salt water to remind us of our tears. If we ate it on a holiday, it was to remind us of centuries of oppression, and make us grateful for what we had.

This is by no means a religious syndrome, though. I'll bet a fair number of children of the sixties and seventies were forced to sit at the dinner table until every trace of food was gone, their parents, like mine, frustrated and enraged: "but you LOVE my peppers stuffed with baloney! Why won't you just eat it? It's midnight for God's sake!"

Two things happened in the postwar world to cause this iron-clad, clean-your-plate dogma of our parents. Diseases like pellagra, rickets, and beriberi made the news in the late fifties - children in the greatest nation in the world were plagued by malnutrition. And India gained its independence from Great Britain. We had to clean our plates because we didn't want to get weird sounding deficiencies, and because there were starving children in India.

One night, while I was grimly stuck at the dinner table, refusing to eat liver and lima beans, my mother told me once again that there were starving children in India (who wouldn't eat a beef liver anyway), and asked if I wanted pellagra.

Me: "Yes!"

I was grateful, relieved she had finally seen the light.

Me: "Pellagra has to taste better than this! Can we order out, or do we have to go get it?"

Mom (wearily): "What is *wrong* with you? Eat your liver. It's got iron in it. Keeps you from getting the anemia."

***

My friend Mark came over to my house for the first time when we were in tenth grade. We immediately scavenged for food. He rummaged through the fridge and cupboards, muttering phrases like, "that doesn't look right" and "weird place to put *that*" and "are there raw onions on everything?"

He found two blue boxes of macaroni and cheese, and with a ruthless efficiency and competence that my mother's kitchen had never seen, set about boiling water and cooking macaroni. When it was done, he dumped it back in the pot. I waited expectantly for the dust packets to be opened.

He went to the fridge, got butter (actually, fake margarine), skim milk, and put them in the macaroni. He sliced open the dust packets, dumped them in, and started mixing. He took two slices of American cheese, unwrapped them, and lay them carefully on top.

Me (horrified): "What the hell are you doing?"

He stirred briskly.

Mark: "This is how you make it."

Me: "Bullshit."

I used the same implacable voice God must have used to say, "No shellfish."

He handed me an empty blue box. I read the back of it: *Milk, butter, cheese dust.*

I took a bowl of the finished product and tasted it. No crunch. It was warm, cheesy, and buttery. It tasted like the picture on the front of the box looked like. It was not orange.

When my mother got home that night, I was at the table with a bowl of the macaroni and cheese Mark had made. I had finished microwaving it when I heard her car pull up in the driveway. She gave me the blank stare she used when she simply had no idea what I was up to.

Mom: "Stace. What's that?"

Me: "Food. Eat it."

She wrinkled her nose.

Mom: "What for?"

Me: "Because there are starving children in India and it'll keep you from getting the rickets."

***

MY MOTHER CAME to my house in Kentucky to visit a year ago, and she brought her sister, Aunt Sissy, with her. The two of them set about cooking as soon as they could, and it was an eye opener.

I have a spice cabinet to the right of the stove. After my divorce, well meaning people bought me housewarming gifts like pots, pans, spices, plates, forks, knives, cookbooks, laundry soap, all-purpose cleaner, and deodorant. If gifts are a nice way of sending silent messages, my friends wanted me to start cooking properly, clean the place up, and smell good.

My daughters had been told stories of the food I had been served as a child and how bad it was. Not coincidentally, it was usually followed by them complaining about whatever I had cooked that day. But sometimes they just wanted me to tell them about some of the more horrific staples, like ghost stories around a campfire.

My Daughters: "The chicken soup! Tell us about the chicken soup!" They shuddered in fearful delight.

The soup was a family classic - my grandmother's recipe. Whenever any of her four children came to visit, the soup was always the first course. It was a broth that trended yellow but never got there, half a carrot sliced lengthwise, a celery stalk, and a small pyramid of chicken bones, right in the middle. No salt, no chicken. At Passover, one festive matzah ball would be added.

My cousins and I all have memories of sitting on the floor of Grandma's small, narrow, post-war GI townhouse in Winfield Park, New Jersey, watching our parents, aunts, and uncles clustered around the small dining table, slurping up Grandma's soup, sucking the bones, and praising her. Because we never knew what came first, the chicken soup or the egg, I didn't know if Grandma made the soup because her kids said they loved it, or if her family said they loved it because she always made it.

Salads were a must on my mother's menu. She believed salads were good for us, so we got them two meals a day. There was a small revolt against the endless salads when our motor home was parked for a year in California, and it saved our lives. My mother did not wash the salad vegetables at all, and poisoned herself with the arsenic that was in use at the time as a pesticide. When she forgets my name, or those of her grandchildren, it is the fault of the arsenic poisoning, as in, "SSSSStace. I got the arsenic poisoning."

What went into Mom's salad? Lettuce, both normal and weird - iceberg, radicchio, spinach. Shaved carrots, celery, and a solid layer of red onions.

She loved red onions. They went on or in everything - eggs, sandwiches, salads, stews, meatloaf, you name it. There was always a big bag in the house.

My mother cooked with two staples - red onions and dust (the cheese dust of boxed mac and cheese, paprika on the roast chicken, bread crumbs on the salmon croquettes, the eggshells that always ended up in the egg salad, and many others). You know you've got her recipe right when there's an overpowering onion flavor, and a tooth grinding crunch. I believe this came from her lifelong smoking habit, and the horse that kicked her in the teeth when she was sixteen. There may have been some taste bud damage, and I think onions and dust were a way to sample what she was eating.

Spices? You guessed it. More dust.

Choosing to grill out the first night of her visit in 2010 was a cowardly thing to do, but grilled meat was simple and easy. The fewer recipes, the better.

Side by side, my mother and her sister worked at the counter next to the sink, prepping meat, a green salad, and my aunt's famous macaroni salad. My daughters, aged 12 and 14, stood in the kitchen to watch the legend come to life. It did not take long.

My mother turned away from the cutting board.

Mom: "Caitlyn. Get me some onions from the pantry. Three or four big ones should do it."

Caitlyn (innocently): "We don't have any onions."

My mother put her half-glasses on so she could peer over them at her, staring her down, her hands dripping wet from washing the salad. Even though we had faced death many times on our move to California – the Grand Canyon, Hoover Dam, unwashed fruit, mountain roads too narrow for our Winnebago – we did learn to wash our vegetables.

Mom: "How can you not have onions? That's disgusting."

Disgusting was an all-purpose word, good for everything from witnessing bestiality to the outrageous price of gasoline.

Erin: "I guess Dad forgot to buy them."

She shook her head sadly.

Erin: "We asked for them, but sometimes he just doesn't listen."

Their grandmother put her arms around their shoulders.

Mom: "He really doesn't. He's just like his father."

Caitlyn: "That son of a bitch."

I stalked into the kitchen, grabbing my car keys. I glared at Erin.

Me: "And to think I told your mother not to drown you in the well when you were born."

I headed for the garage.

Mom: "Get a whole bag! I can't believe you don't have onions in the house!"

Erin (happily): "It's disgusting!"

The three of them stood together in the kitchen in a tight cluster, a coven formed around my lamentable incompetence and lack of foresight, awaiting one last unspeakable ingredient for their noxious cauldron.

I was back in twenty minutes. I held the bag of onions out to my mother and glared at my children, who beamed at me from behind her back with a dewy eyed innocence.

Me (acidly): "This is on you. I don't want to hear it when you're hungry later."

Mom: "SSSSStace. What are you talking about? What is *wrong* with you?"

She didn't wait for an answer and I knew better than to offer one. She had been asking what was wrong with me my whole life. It was rhetorical.

She went back to the cutting board and began chopping onions. My kids, who stood nearby to help, wept openly. Soon there were onion flecks in their hair and on their clothes from all the frenzied chopping. My mother remained dry eyed from years of accumulated tolerance. Onions went in the hamburger meat, formed the top layer of the green salad, and were dumped by the handful into the macaroni salad my aunt was silently and expertly making. She knew better than to argue and just mixed them in.

I wandered into the kitchen in time to see the finale. Without looking, my mother reached into the spice rack, grabbed a jar, unscrewed the lid, and went to dump it into her sister's macaroni salad.

My aunt grabbed her wrist just in time.

Aunt Sissy: "Carol! What is that?"

My mother put her glasses on and peered at the label on the jar.

Mom: "Crystallized ginger."

Aunt Sissy (drily): "In macaroni salad."

Mom: "It has a nice taste."

Aunt Sissy: "No it doesn't."

Mom: "You won't taste it, Sis. It doesn't taste like anything."

Aunt Sissy: "So why put it in?"

My mother stared blankly at her.

Mom (as if speaking to an idiot): "Sis. It has a nice taste, I said. Why don't you listen?"

My aunt physically covered the bowl of macaroni salad with her arms.

Aunt Sissy: "Carol. Put it away."

My mother did, but rooted around the spice rack some more.

Mom (triumphantly): "Oregano! Dill weed! Tarragon! Cinnamon!"

Aunt Sissy: "No. No. No. Stop already."

My children looked at me, panic rising in their red, teary eyes. I leaned casually against the fridge, arms folded.

Me: "When's dinner gonna be ready? I'm starving!"

9

LEFT FOR DEAD

THE SUMMER OF 1979 was a disaster.

Our above-ground swimming pool had been demolished to make way for the parking lot my mother needed for her beauty salon. She was ending her relationship with Bernie the Disco Prince (who we liked because he stayed entirely out of our way) and she was being sued by Bill the Stoner because she ran him over with her car the year before. Ted the Lightbulb Salesman was sniffing around to replace Bernie the Disco Prince in my mother's affections. There was something about him that made me fear for my future.

The impending lawsuit caused my mother to blurt things out at odd moments like a first-year law student with Tourette's syndrome:

Mom: "Pre-trial motion? How about my car running his ass over? There's your pre-trial motion - thirty miles an hour!"

Mom: "They can cram their deposition up their ass. What's a deposition?"

Mom: "I'm all the goddamn witness they need. Witness list. My tuchus has a witness list!"

Mom: "Discovery? What's to discover? A druggie who can't pedal fast enough?"

Sometimes she would bolt to the phone, dial as furiously as she could (considering it was a rotary dialer) and speak:

Mom: "I need him dead. You hear me? Dead. Wiped out!"

Uncle George the Bastard was a police lieutenant in his final year before retirement. There was no way he was going to assassinate Bill the Stoner, but we didn't know that; we were terrified of him.

Uncle George the Bastard: "Who is this?"

Mom: "George. What do you mean, 'who is this'? You know who it is!"

Uncle George the Bastard: "A dozen women have called me today asking to have some guy killed. You'll have to be more specific."

Mom: "Put my sister on the phone."

Mom: "Sis. I don't need this shit. I need George to wipe this guy out. Does he think he's being funny? Is he some kind of smart guy? Why did you have to marry a goy?"

Sissy: "You married a goy."

Mom: "I didn't keep him, Sis. I threw the son of a bitch out. Your husssssband married into this family. He should help the family!"

Sissy: "Carol. We're not Italian."

Mom: "Sis. What are you talking about? I know we're not Italian!"

Sissy: "You want him to kill someone."

Mom: "If I lose this case I'm coming to live with you!"

Bill the Stoner was never closer to death than at that moment, even when you count the time my mother, trying to light a cigarette and change the radio station at the same time, ran him over with her car.

***

My Aunt Sissy lived about two miles away and had a huge in-ground pool. It occurred to me that we could move our water-based operations over there now that there were cars parked where our pool had been. I suggested to Layne the Favorite that he ask our mother to let us ride our bikes to Aunt Sissy's to go swimming. She agreed in a flash; not only was the favorite son asking, but an afternoon of us invading Sissy's home would be a precursor of what was to come if Bill the Stoner took our house away. One day with us and my aunt would send her husband out into the night with one of the unregistered pistols he had taken from some criminal or other to hunt down Bill the Stoner and make him disappear.

We set out to bike to Aunt Sissy's house the next morning as if we were the first settlers to colonize the moon: we had packed every conceivable thing into our backpacks - towels, spare clothes, my dad's golf shoes, baseball caps, sunscreen, orange juice, ceramic figurines my mother thought would look nice in her sister's living room, my father's spare bowling balls, and snacks, which were tupperware containers of onion-laden salads and my mother's famous cream cheese sandwiches.

The recipe: soy based cream cheese, brown bread made from dried spinach flour. It tasted like the absence of hope.

She had dialed her sister up on the rotary phone a few minutes earlier to warn her that we were coming.

Mom: "Figurines!" She often started phone conversations in mid-thought and just expected the listener to know what she was talking about.

Sissy: "What? Who is this?"

Mom: "Sis. I'm sending the kids. With the figurines."

Sissy: "What figurines?"

Mom: "Sis. The figurinessssss! And Fred's golf shoes. For George."

Sissy: "George doesn't golf."

Mom: "They're nice shoes."

Sissy: "He doesn't wear Fred's size."

Mom: "Sis. They're nice shoes! I also put Fred's cracked balls in there. Son of a bitch."

Uncle George the Bastard never kept any of my father's old stuff that my mother sent over. They had been best friends long before they met and married these sisters. No matter how good the shoes were, even if he played golf and wore the right size, it was still like walking around in a dead man's suit. I found out years later that he carefully boxed up all this detritus my mother sent and took it to Dad's house when my father was at work. Every now and then my dad would find a box on his porch when he came home, stuffed with the things he had believed were gone forever. It was one of the many reasons I admired Uncle George the Bastard.

We lined our bikes up in the paved backyard and strapped on the backpacks, which felt like they were stuffed with rocks. The

air was still. We took a deep breath before this momentous journey over great distances. We were boys about to become men, on
our first independent trip away from home on flimsy, wheel-borne
death traps. Her little boys were growing up.

Mom: "Don't pee in the pool. Your uncle will beat your ass if you do.
You know what a bastard he is."

I want to be at the launch of the rocket that carries the first human
colonists into space, just so I can send them off with just that kind of stir-
ring speech.

Me: "It's a long way…"

Mom: "Give her the figurines as soon as you walk in the door. I don't
want them broken. And the shoes!"

Me: "We could be gone all day. We could get hit by a car…"

Mom: "Don't drop your father's balls. They're already cracked as it is."

Our neighbor Jimmy the Third called down from his favorite perch
inside his upper-story window, a disembodied voice from on high, like God.

Jimmy the Third: "Bowling balls in their backpacks, Carol? Are
they joining the Marines?"

Mom: "Jasper! They're for my sister's husband! He's a real bastard!"

Jimmy the Third: "Jimmy!"

Mom: "That's what I said!"

Layne the Favorite was covered in sweat before we went ten feet. He
had the cracked bowling balls in his pack. The ceramic figurines in my

backpack clinked as we set off. One of them busted open my salad. To this day the stench of raw onions and fake cheese is the smell of adventure.

* * *

MY BROTHER RODE faster than me (even weighted down with the bowling balls) and was soon a spot far away in the distance. I kept yelling at him to stop and wait, but he either ignored me or didn't hear. Soon enough I was alone, pedaling laboriously, reeking of onions, and the ceramics in my backpack grinding against each other.

I was riding in the street along a line of parked cars. I stood up to pedal faster, lost my balance when my heavy pack shifted, and the front tire of my bike hit the back bumper of a Pontiac. I flew headfirst over the handlebars and hit the back window with my face. I slid off the car and down to the ground, landing spread-eagled on my back, crushing the figurines to shards. My juice bottle shattered, and I lay between two parked cars, orange juice and salad dressing soaking into my shirt, pointy bits of ceramics sticking out of my skin, my father's empty golf shoes near my head. The only pain free spot was where the flattened cream cheese sandwiches pressed against me.

When I came to, it was nearly dark. I had lain for most of the afternoon in the street with my bike on top of me. I got to my feet. One side of my face was numb, and my head felt full of rocks. I bent over to pick up my bike and nearly vomited. I leaned against the car to steady myself and slowly started walking my bike toward home. I left the reeking backpack on the ground. Going that one mile took nearly an hour. The front wheel of the bike was bent from the impact and the smell of orange-infused, cream-cheesy onions made me have to stop to gag, tears running down my face. By the time I made it to the back steps of my house, it was fully dark.

A high powered flashlight beam lit up my bike. A voice called down to me from a third-story window:

Jimmy the Third: "How's it goin, Sport?"

Me: "About the same as always."

Jimmy the Third: "That bike of yours is all busted up again."

I was not easy on bikes. From his high altitude platform, Jimmy the Third had seen every accident I'd had over the years. He would come down after I went inside, take my bike back to his garage, and return it the next day good as new. He knew my mother would never get me a new one, and I would have to wait for Layne the Favorite to want a replacement for his so I could get the hand-me-down.

Jimmy the Third: "At least you still got your clothes on."

I used to ride my bike naked. When I was five. Neighbors never forget the little things. I dropped my bike and staggered inside. Mom and Layne the Favorite were in our basement on the couch, in front of the TV. Layne the Favorite was eating a McDonald's hamburger. There was a half full white bag with the golden arches logo next to him. I must have hit my head pretty hard - my mother did not tolerate fast food in the house.

Me: "I'm home."

Mom: "About time! You need to get yourself to bed, Buster."

Me: "Layne. Have fun swimming?"

Layne the Favorite (mouth full): "Yep."

Me: "Did you notice that I wasn't there with you?"

Layne the Favorite looked at me, shrugged, and reached into the bag for another french fry.

Me: "On your way home, did you see me? Behind the Pontiac?"

He shook his head and kept eating.

Me: "Do you remember smelling onions and orange juice? Around the halfway point toward home?"

Layne the Favorite: "I thought that was me."

Me: "And McDonald's? We never get McDonald's! Did you think I was dead? Is this my funeral?"

Mom: "What are you talking about? Your brother was hungry!"

Me: "Can I have some?"

My mother looked at Layne the Favorite. He pondered, weighing this treat against whatever glimmer of guilt he may have felt for leaving me to die. He shook his head, jammed a fistful of fries into his mouth, and glared defiantly at the glowing TV screen.

Mom: "You shouldn't eat this close to bedtime anyway."

Me: "I'm not sure I should go to bed. I hit my head pretty hard on a Pontiac's butt. I might have a concussion."

Mom: "What? Pontiac's don't have butts. What is *wrong* with you?"

Me (speaking as slowly and clearly as I could): "For one thing, I hit my head pretty hard. On a parked car."

Me: (indignantly): "Then was left to die."

Me (with slurred speech): "I have returned, apparently still alive."

Me (weakly): "Huzzah!"

Mom: "SSSStace. You're so dramatic. Just like your father."

Me: "Maybe I will go to bed."

Mom: "Good idea. Ted's coming over."

Layne the Favorite stared at her in surprise, his lips shiny with grease, crusty with salt.

Layne the Favorite: "What's he coming over for?"

Mom: "He's going to help me with something."

Layne the Favorite: "I don't want him to come over now. What do you need him for?"

Mom: "Layner. He's coming to help me with my court case. That goddamned lawsuit. You know? That druggie who's suing me? Ted said he could do something about it."

Bill the Stoner, if you're reading this, I'd love to hear from you, buddy. Just so I know you're okay. Drop me a line.

If you can.

10

TRAILER TRASH

How did I become trailer trash? I fell for the oldest trick in the book.

I use it now on my own kids:

Me: "Get in the car."

Kids: "Where are we going?"

Me: "Just get in the car."

This happened in the spring of 1980. Ted the Drug Dealer, still only Ted the Lightbulb Salesman back then, was around all the time. He didn't live with us because we had moved into our half finished basement as if we were hiding out from the secret agents of an oppressive regime. I'm sure he had a place somewhere, but like the third floor apartment in our house, I never saw it.

We all piled in the car (Ted the Lightbulb Salesman's Cadillac) and drove for an hour on the Garden State Parkway. Layne the Favorite, used to getting much more information from my mother, was becoming more and more frantic about not knowing where we were going and why. Years later, the whispers I heard throughout the family were that Ted the Drug Dealer finally left because he was tired of competing with Layne the Favorite.

My mother had the same problem when she married her fourth husband, Marvin, King of the Jews, who was obsessed with how old Layne the Favorite was. It was his favorite conversation starter. I had fun with it:

Marvin, King of the Jews: "Your brutha's what, twenty-two?"

Me: "Twenty-two years, eight months, three days, six hours, fifteen minutes. Wait. Sixteen minutes."

Marvin, King of the Jews: "Old enough to move out already, right? I'm just saying."

Me: "I don't know, Marvin. I moved out when I was seventeen, but it's not for everyone. I read somewhere that kids are living at home longer, even into their thirties and forties. Some never leave."

Marvin, King of the Jews (squeakily): "Never?"

Me (solemnly): "Never ever."

Me: "Marvin? You don't look so good. Where're your pills?"

Me: "Here, take this glass of water. Hold the pill under your tongue. Breathe, Marvin, breathe. In, out, in, out. Come on, stay with me."

Me: "Okay, I'm gonna thump you on the back to try and get you breathing again. It might leave a bruise, but here goes."

Me: "That seemed to work, but your face is the color of an eggplant."

Mom: "Eggplant? I can make eggplant for dinner if you want."

Me and Marvin, King of the Jews: "NO!"

Mom: "But you love my eggplant!"

Me: "Nice to have you back, Marvin. Did you see a light or a tunnel or anything?"

Marvin, King of the Jews: "Almost twenty-three years old."

Me: "He will be. Only three months, twenty-six days, eighteen hours, and forty-three minutes from now. Hold on. Forty-two minutes."

Mom (her teeth gritted): "Stop talking about how old he is!"

* * *

LAYNE THE FAVORITE (circa 1980): "Ma. Where are we going?"

He asked this question lots of times on the course of the drive. Every time he did, my mother would look at Ted the Lightbulb Salesman and he would shake his head. So she did her best to soothe my brother.

Mom: "Try not to worry, Layner. It's not bad. You'll see."

He turned to me.

Layne the Favorite: "Where do you think we're going?"

I had no idea. Ted the Lightbulb Salesman was not a big explainer of things. He was the kind of guy who would just suddenly get up and start moving. The only hint we'd get about his intent or destination was whatever he was carrying in his hands. Some examples:

1. A tennis racquet.
2. His .22 pistol.

3. A mason jar full of gasoline.
4. A plastic garbage bag full of marijuana and his machete.
5. A bag of coin wrappers and three drawstring bags.

It was like a game of Clue, in which after he became "Ted the Drug Dealer", the answer would be, "Ted the Drug Dealer, in the kitchen, with four hundred pounds of marijuana," or, "Ted the Drug Dealer, on the side of the road, with the drawstring bags and his stepson, picking up loose change that had spilled out on the ground after he beat up the fare in his cab who tried to stiff him."

Circa spring, 1980, we pulled into the driveway of a small house near New Brunswick. Parked on the grass to one side of the driveway was a ten-year old Winnebago. It looked quiet and innocent, sitting there in the late afternoon sunlight. Maybe it didn't become the bane of one's existence until you started it up with the key. Perhaps the demons who lived in it needed to warm up before they could unleash their evil upon the world.

Maybe it always was just a plain old slightly worn recreational vehicle. Maybe.

The owner of the Winnebago was what I call Classic Catholic Man: a large, mostly silent giant who had a sacred room in the house that was all his own; his many children dared not to cross the threshold unless summoned for punishment, and his wife would enter only to clean it up (when he was not in it) or to bring him food and drink. He was the unquestioned master of his domain, able to sit in moody silence in front of his giant television while the hue and cry of his wife and brood went on in other parts of the house without him.

My Uncle George the Bastard was one of these. He lent me the money to buy my first house. The man I bought my current residence from was also a Classic Catholic Man. This is more than an interesting coincidence – apparently I get my homes from these guys. In the case of the most recent one, I still get his mail from some of the many Catholic organizations he belonged to. I know it's wrong to open other people's mail, even if they moved out nearly a decade ago, but I did once. It was a newsletter, so I felt okay about violating his privacy. The titles of the articles in it were fascinating:

1. ***Your TV Room: Sanctum Sanctorum***
2. ***Dinner by Six: There's No Excuse***
3. ***New Appliances: Convenience or Cop-Out?***
4. ***Warm Up Before Beating the Kids – Muscle Cramps Can Detract from Proper Discipline***
5. ***Ten Reasons Why No One Can Ever Sit in Your Chair – Ever***

His wife met us at the front door and asked us to come in. She was a tiny, thin woman with a lined face and swollen, red hands. Eight small children, ranging in age from five to twelve clustered, not quite out of sight, lurking above our heads on the stairs leading to the second floor, peering intently at us. It was like being in a Dickensian orphanage; I wished I had brought some gruel or socks or something for them. If they tried to pick my pocket, I would let them, the poor little things.

Mrs. Classic Catholic Man (checking the clock on the kitchen wall): "It will be a few minutes. ABC Sports ends at five."

At that moment, the refrigerator howled and the dishwasher groaned. Water flooded from the dishwasher's outlet hose into the sink.

Mom: "You need a new dishwasher."

Mrs. Classic Catholic Man looked at Ted the Lightbulb Salesman anxiously.

Mom: "There's something not right about that. It shouldn't be shooting water into the sink. Probably a new Frigidaire too."

Mrs. Classic Catholic Man blinked furiously a few times.

Mrs. Classic Catholic Man (addressing Ted the Lightbulb Salesman): "Your wife is very sweet, but Henry just bought the new projection television. It's the best way to watch boxing. He says it's like being there."

Mom: "We're not married."

Ted the Lightbulb Salesman: "I don't watch sports."

Layne the Favorite: "I want to see the big TV!"

Mrs. Classic Catholic Man paled, and she fell back against the kitchen table. One of its legs made a loud cracking sound and the table listed to one side.

Mrs. Classic Catholic Man (shrieking): "Henry! The people are here to look at the Winnebago!"

The children on the stairs drew a collective gasp. All eyes turned to the dark-paneled wall off the kitchen, where a solitary door was closed tight. I could hear the sounds of some sporting event from the TV – oxen races, tiddly balls, synchronized clowning. Possibly soccer. I didn't watch sports either, so I couldn't identify it.

The doorknob turned slowly, and the door started to open.

Smallest Child on the Stairs (squeaking): "But it's not five o'clock, Mother!"

Mrs. Classic Catholic Man, her face tight with anxiety, flapped her hand at the interruption. "Shhhhhhhhh!" she hissed. That little girl was likely going to bed gruel-less that night for her backsass. Good news, though – while getting spanked in the Sanctum Sanctorum, she could get caught up on the latest tiddly ball scores, or see how the oxen races turned out. Watching TV in color was a rare treat for the children, even if they had to get smacked to do it. I imagined some of the younger ones took turns getting in trouble just so they could watch the big TV for a few minutes:

1. Mary Katherine: "It's your turn. Go move Father's newspaper an inch to the right. Maybe you'll get to see a McDonald's commercial!"
2. Mary Simona: "You're up. Remember your line: 'Father, I want to be a scientist when I grow up.' Say it with me. With feeling!"
3. Henry Christopher: "Walk right in, take the remote control, and change the channel. Fear slows you down! Don't hesitate!"
4. Henry William: "Say, 'I think Jimmy Carter is the best President we ever had.' It's the only way you'll get to see the whole boxing match, and you know it."
5. Henry Henry: "You have to let Father see you hugging that strange little boy from down the street. I know it's awkward, but you need to hold him for more than two seconds this time! Is five minutes of TV good enough for you, or do you want more? Tighten up already!"

Henry, Classic Catholic Man came out. Behind him the glow from the TV lit up the room like a small sun. He was huge, both tall and wide, clad in a white T-shirt, baggy gray sweatpants, white socks, and brown sandals. His belly was a solid slope of intractable fat that started below his third chin and ended deep in the front of his sweatpants like a barely submerged volcano. There was silver stubble on his red face, lining the fleshy hills and valleys of his cheeks and chins like freshly-planted stalks of wheat. His eyes were small, ice-blue and watery. He stalked over to Ted the Lightbulb Salesman and shook his hand.

Henry, Classic Catholic Man: "You Ted?"

Ted the Lightbulb Salesman (nodding): "This is Carol, and —"

Henry, Classic Catholic Man: "It's outside. Let's go look at it."

He went to the door and we followed. He put the key in the Winnebago's side door and opened it. Behind the outer door was a screen that had to be opened as well. Then he bent down, grunting, and unhooked the metal step, lowering it.

Henry, Classic Catholic Man turned and looked at Ted, doing a double take when he saw my mother and us with him.

Henry, Classic Catholic Man: "Find out what they want and then we can take it for a test drive."

Ted the Ligtbulb Salesman: "They're coming with us."

Henry, Classic Catholic Man: "They are?"

Mom: "Of course we are. I'm not going to buy this thing without making sure it's right. I work too hard for my money to buy something sight unssssssssseeen. You know?"

Henry, Classic Catholic Man gazed at her, silent for what seemed like a full minute.

Henry, Classic Catholic Man: "You have money?" he asked. "Of your own?"

Mom: "Don't be silly. Of course I have money. I have my own businessssssssss."

Quick as a flash, she produced one of her business cards and held it out to him.

Mom: "I'm a cosmetologist."

He stared at the card.

Henry, Classic Catholic Man: "You're going to predict my future?"

She huffed.

Mom: "Cosmetologist. Hair dresssssssser."

She looked at Ted, her eyes wide.

Mom (scornfully): "Goyim."

And back to Henry.

Mom: "You could use a trim. And a facial."

She looked him up and down critically, her face creased with disdain.

Mom: "I can predict your future, too, Harry. Probably a heart attack or something like that. A stroke. You're way too zaftig. You know? Zaftig?"

Henry fled into the Winnebago. We followed.

I was taken in by the motor home right away. It was just the thing a kid could love. Everything was miniature - the fridge, the table that folded down between the two bench seats to make a couch, the two rear bunks with cunning storage bays under the mattresses, the tiny bathroom and shower stall. It was a little house. There was a bigger bed over the driver and passenger seats in the front that lowered on a clever hinge so you could climb up into it.

I was sold.

Keep in mind that, at the time, my bedroom was the right angle of the basement left over from where they put the furnace in, and I slept on a fold out couch. With my brother.

When my kids watched Harry Potter for the first time, they were horrified that he had been forced to live in a small room under the stairs.

Me: "Oh, please. That thing's a palace."

***

CIRCA SPRING, 1980, Henry, Classic Catholic Man settled into the enormous driver's seat of the Winnebago and started it up. I knew as much about engines as I did about sports, but I detected a whining, gasping noise before the engine churned to life. I was going to suggest to Ted the Lightbulb Salesman that maybe there was something wrong with the plutonium nugget or the paddlewheel or whatever made the Winnebago move, but I held my tongue. It seemed to be what Henry would have wanted, and he was busy driving a house, for God's sake. Best he be left to it without interruption.

Twenty-five years later, I read an article in one of the Catholic magazines on this very subject:

"Seen But Not Heard" Series, Part Two: Motorcycles, Boats, and Motor Homes

I was delighted. The little house on wheels actually drove! We went back on to the Garden State Parkway and cruised around for a while. I sat at the little table with Layne the Favorite and my mother, looking rapturously out the big window at tiny passing cars. Whenever I saw another kid my own age fidgeting in the cramped back seat of a seventies-style car, I shot him or her a little salute that said, "That's right. Riding in a house. A _house_. Sucker!"

If Henry, Classic Catholic Man would have been willing to acknowledge my existence, he would have pointed out that pride was a sin.

I felt like Dorothy on her way to Oz. Houses as a mode of travel. It was brilliant.

Me: "We should get a little dog."

Mom: "Your brother doesn't like little dogs."

She looked at Layne the Favorite.

Mom: "Do you like the motor home, Layner?"

He was a bit put out at not having been privy to this plan.

Layne the Favorite: "I don't know. It's weird riding in a house."

Me: "It's great!"

My mother shushed me.

Mom: "Think about it, honey. It'll be fun! It's like camping!"

Note for future reference: It is *nothing* like camping. Or fun.

In the end, we bought the Winnebago. Henry, Classic Catholic Man used the proceeds to put in one of the very first surround sound systems in his neighborhood. We were also to thank for the new barbecue grill that only *he* was allowed to use when his friends (other Classic Catholic Men) came over. Ten percent - you guessed it - to the church.

Two months later, my mother announced we were moving to California. She added that it was just so convenient - now that we had the motor home, we could spend the summer traveling across the country in it. What a fortunate coincidence!

I started to feel as though I had been had, as if there was some sort of long term plan that I was not privy to.

The last Catholic Man newsletter that came in the mail held all the answers:

Your Plans For Others: No One's Business But Yours

11

DEATH AT HOOVER DAM

THE WINNEBAGO WE lived in broke down for the first time a week before we nearly died at Hoover Dam. Ted the Lightbulb Salesman set himself on fire while trying to fix it.

We had left New Jersey in early June, 1980 with Ted the Lightbulb Salesman at the RV's helm. My mother was his navigator and co-pilot, sitting to his right, with a map of the United States folded in her lap. Layne the Favorite was in his bunk, across the aisle from mine, outside the door to the bathroom. I had a pile of books to read. He had a Sony Walkman that no one was allowed to touch. No one.

On the morning we left home, we sat in the Winnebago- which was parked in our driveway - in silence. I had a sense of a great impending moment - the only house I had ever known, empty behind us. My child-hood friends lingering near the cherry tree - Jimmy the Fourth and Kevin the Weak-Bladdered, watching. Before us, the open road: three thousand miles to California. In Ted the Lightbulb Salesman's hand, the key. How many pioneers had sat mute for a few seconds on the cusp of a life chang-ing journey, awaiting only the incoming tide, the crack of a whip, the spin of a propeller, the roar of a rocket's thrusters, the start of the ignition?

Ted the Lightbulb Salesman turned the key. Nothing happened.

Layne the Favorite: "Great."

The rivalry with Ted the Lightbulb Salesman over who my mother liked best had begun. Layne the Favorite did not know he had already won, but Ted the Lightbulb Salesman didn't know it either, so the battle was joined.

Layne the Favorite: "Good job, Ted."

Mom: "What the hell, Ted?"

Poor bastard. I wanted to remind him of a few things:

1. He was there voluntarily—I was the victim of a biological crap shoot.
2. The Winnebago was his idea.
3. Layne the Favorite was always and forever the favorite.
4. His navigator didn't know how to unfold the map, let alone read it.
5. He had the Winnebago's gas tank switched over to auxiliary.
6. The auxiliary gas tank was empty.

But I didn't bother. Eventually Ted the Lightbulb Salesman figured it out.

The first part of the trip was pretty good: school was out for three months, I was getting to see parts of the country I had learned about in class, Layne the Favorite was busy with his Walkman and plotting Ted the Lightbulb Salesman's ultimate defeat, and my mother was in map reading boot camp:

Ted the Lightbulb Salesman: "North or south on 81?"

Mom: "How the hell should I know?"

Ted the Lightbulb Salesman: "Read the map."

Mom: "It's not on the map."

Ted the Lightbulb Salesman: "Interstate 81 is missing from the map of the United States?"

Mom: "Shut up, Ted."

Layne the Favorite cackled at that. I reminded him that this trip, for all intents and purposes, was their honeymoon - they had married two weeks before and had spent the rest of the time packing up all our earthly belongings. He looked positively giddy at the news.

We had to pull our monstrosity of a motor home over quite often so that Ted the Lightbulb Salesman could read the map.

Ted the Lightbulb Salesman: "Found it! Interstate 81. Eisenhower will be so relieved he didn't forget to build it."

Mom: "Ted. What are you talking about? Eisenhower's dead. What is *wrong* with you?"

Uh oh. That was the question she always asked me. Ted the Lightbulb Salesman was doomed.

The eastern United States passed without much comment. My brother and I spent our time figuring out our new lives - reading books, napping, listening to music, looking out the window. My mother was trying to remember eighth grade geography while looking at the map. Ted the Lightbulb Salesman was learning how to pilot a huge vehicle on American roads.

The most exciting thing about the first week was when we approached the Mississippi River. Like other pioneers in ages past, once you crossed the Mississippi, you were locked in, even if it meant you had to shoot your favorite horse in the head or eat the other members of your caravan. There was no going back.

We watched out the window at the approach. At last, I would see the mighty river and look for rafts piloted by fugitive juvenile delinquents.

I could see a bridge out the window. This was it...

The bridge crossed over a relatively unimpressive river.

Ted the Lightbulb Salesman looked at it and commented: "That's the Mississippi River? I piss more than that."

A few miles later we encountered the behemoth body of water and spent what seemed like an hour driving over it.

Ted the Lightbulb Salesman: "Oh."

✳ ✳ ✳

THE WINNEBAGO'S ENGINE started to whine almost immediately after crossing the state line from Oklahoma into Texas.

Mom: "Are you sure this highway goes all the way to California?"

Ted the Lightbulb Salesman (wearily): "It's on the map."

Mom: "Ted. I haven't unfolded that part yet."

Ted the Lightbulb Salesman: "Shut up, Carol."

Layne the Favorite: "Hey! Don't talk to my mother like that!"

Me: "Especially on your honeymoon."

Ted the Lightbulb Salesman: "Everybody quiet down! There's something wrong with the RV."

He pulled over to the side of the road. Alongside the interstate ran a post fence strung with barbed wire. We all gathered outside, near the fence, in the overwhelming Texas heat.

Layne the Favorite: "How far does this fence go?"

Me: "At least as far as the fold in the map."

My mother stared at me blankly. "SSSSSSSSStace. What is *wrong* with you?"

Ted the Lightbulb Salesman looked at me with sudden alarm on his face. I nodded solemnly at him. Time to form a club, establish by-laws, and have some matching jackets made. He went back to the RV and climbed in. As his fellow pariah, I tagged along.

The top of the Winnebago's engine was hidden under a latched trap door between the driver and passenger seats. The trap door was covered by an ugly yellow seventies-style shag carpet. He opened it up. We both peered at the engine. Nothing happened.

He sat in the driver's seat and turned the key. The engine squealed and whined, but didn't start. It shook in its housings between the seats. Ted switched the gas tank selector from Main to Auxilliary and back, but our RV never fell for the same trick twice. Even I knew that wasn't going to work, and I was nine years old and thought the Winnebago ran on fissionable material.

Ted the Lightbulb Salesman got up from the chair and went past me, out the door, and around to the trailer we were towing behind the motor home. He opened it and rummaged around. My mother and Layne the Favorite stared at me.

Even though she was a foot away from Ted the Lightbulb Salesman, my mother asked me: "SSSSSStace. What's he doing?"

I shrugged. For all I knew he had a spare plutonium nugget or whatever the engine ran on stored in the trailer. I was just looking forward to the next fold in the map.

**

I<small>T</small> <small>WAS</small> <small>TOO</small> hot to stay outside while Ted the Lightbulb Salesman did whatever he was doing. And since he never explained anything to us, we didn't hang around to help him. He came back inside with a mason jar of liquid and ordered my mother into the driver's seat.

Mom: "Ted. You want me to drive? It won't start."

Ted the Lightbulb Salesman: "Just turn the key when I tell you."

He fiddled with something in the engine, told her to turn the key, and started pouring the liquid from the jar into the motor. I stood up and moved toward the door.

The engine caught and turned over. A puff of black smoke shot up to the ceiling. Ted the Lightbulb Salesman's hand and the mason jar caught fire. I opened the door.

Mom (coughing): "Ted! What's in the jar?"

Ted the Lightbulb Salesman (surprisingly calm): "Gasoline."

Then he bolted past me, his forearm aflame, and out the door that I held open for him. It was the least I could do - we were now members of the same club. Plus, he was on fire.

Ted the Lightbulb Salesman flung the mason jar of lit gasoline away from him. It smashed against one of the wooden fence posts, igniting the post and the grass under it. He dropped to the ground and rolled around with his arm under himself to put the fire out. He got back up, his forearm hairless and a bit pink, but otherwise unharmed.

The fence post fire was now getting higher. Passing cars were starting to slow down.

Ted the Lightbulb Salesman: "We need to get out of here."

Me: "Seriously? You just set Texas on fire. We're going to be on the news."

Ted the Lightbulb Salesman: "Or in jail."

Me: "Good point. Let's go."

It was too late. Over the roar of the fire we could hear sirens.

***

TED THE LIGHTBULB Salesman's first run-in with the law (and mine) went like this:

Two Texas state troopers got out of their car. They were each six foot five and three hundred pounds, wearing mirrored sunglasses, ten-gallon hats, and carrying pearl-handled revolvers. I thought they were robots. They ran past me with fire extinguishers, put the fire out, set the extinguishers on the ground, and rounded on Ted the Lightbulb Salesman, hands on their gun butts.

Texas Robot Trooper 1: "Sir. Did you start this fire?"

I looked over at the glittering shards of the mason jar at the base of the blackened fence post, Ted the Lightbulb Salesman's burned arm, and the dissipating cloud of black smoke belching from the open door of our RV. I suspected the Texas Robot Troopers needed a software upgrade.

Ted the Lightbulb Salesman: "I had to prime the engine to get it started."

So that's what that was. Priming the engine. One mystery solved, but others remained. For example, what was the plutonium nugget for? Did it just run the lights or something?

Texas Robot Trooper 2: "Is your vehicle running now, sir?"

I looked at the exhaust billowing from the tailpipe of the RV and listened to the sound of the engine. Need for robot software upgrade confirmed.

Ted the Lightbulb Salesman: "I think we're good."

Texas Robot Trooper 1: "Then be on your way, sir. And don't start any more fires."

Good safety tip. Thanks, Texas Robot Troopers.

✳✳✳

SLIGHTLY PAST THE next fold in the map, a few days later, was Hoover Dam.

Mom: "Layner! Come up here! We're getting close to the dam!"

Layne the Favorite went to the front of the RV. My mother pointed her camera out the window and started snapping pictures. We crested the hill of the two lane road we were on and saw it: the towering dam and majestic Lake Mead behind a low stone wall. It was quite a sight.

I smelled something burning. Ted the Lightbulb Salesman was standing upright instead of sitting in the driver's seat. The RV wobbled over the thin yellow line separating us from oncoming traffic. My mother snapped picture after picture.

Me: "What's on fire now?"

Ted the Lightbulb Salesman (surprisingly calm): "The brakes."

***

TED THE ARSONIST struggled to hold the RV on our side of the road as we careened down the hill toward Lake Mead. He stood on the brakes and fought the wheel as we went faster and faster. I heard the tires squeal. My mother kept taking pictures.

Mom: "Ted! Slow down! All my pictures will be blurry!"

Ted the Arsonist: "And wet."

Me: "Wet? Why wet?"

Ted the Arsonist (surprisingly calm): "If I can't get us to stop, we're going in the lake."

Mom: "Ted. What is *wrong* with you? And what's burning?" Click, click, click. "This is disgusting. These are going to be shitty pictures. Thanks a lot, Ted."

Ted the Arsonist: "Carol. The brakes are on fire."

Mom: "No they're not." Click, click, click.

Ted the Arsonist managed to stop the RV when the road we were on bottomed out and started uphill. He found a turn off and pulled over to the side. We all got out and clustered at the wall separating us from Lake Mead. The air was redolent with burning metal and boiled brake fluid (I looked it up - brakes apparently use some sort of fluid for something or other).

Mom: "Ted. Why are we stopping here? The dam's over there."

I glanced at Ted the Arsonist.

Me: "So you can get some better pictures."

Ted's face was a deep purple color. I suspected the honeymoon was not going well.

Mom: "About damn time! I couldn't get a good shot with the way you were driving."

Ted the Arsonist: "Carol! The fucking brakes were on fire!"

She stared at him.

Mom: "So how did we stop, then, smarty pants?"

Ted the Arsonist: "The road started going uphill."

Mom: "What if you couldn't have stopped?"

Ted the Arsonist: "We would have ended up in the lake."

Me: "That's no big deal. We can all swim."

Ted the Arsonist (shaking his head): "Doesn't matter. The turbines will suck you under and grind you up into little bits."

Me: "Wow. Good thing we were able to stop."

Mom: "SSSSSStace. If we were gonna die, that was it. When it's your time to go, it's your time to go."

Me: "Well, we made it out alive. Better luck next time."

While we waited for mobile RV repair, my mother thought it would be a good idea to take the tour of the dam. After going down several levels, our guide took us to a cavernous space with shiny metal spinning things.

Mom: "What are those?"

Hoover Dam Guide (proudly): "Those are the turbines."

Mom: "SSSSSStace. Did you just pee your pants?"

Me: "I fell in a puddle. Can we get out of here now?"

✳ ✳ ✳

NEXT ON THE itinerary was a boat tour of Lake Mead. Layne the Favorite and I had to wear lifejackets along with all of the kids on the boat.

Mom: "I don't know why they put those stupid life vests on the kids. It won't keep the turbines from sucking them down and grinding them up."

Adjacent Mother (clutching her daughter close to her): "Wait. What? Is something wrong with the boat? What was that about the turbines?"

Mom: "Nothing to worry about. When it's your time to go, it's your time to go."

The woman and her daughter got off the boat before it launched.

After we toured the lake, the captain asked if I wanted to take a turn at steering. In retrospect, it sounded like an irresponsible thing to do, but it was 1980. Safety was something the robots in Texas worried about - this was Nevada.

I jumped at the chance. All I did was stand there with the wheel in my hand, holding the boat straight. I noticed we were on a collision course with the dam, but I was used to such things by then. Besides, someone more nautically qualified was bound to take over when we no longer needed to go in a straight line.

The captain grabbed the microphone he had been using to narrate the tour.

Irresponsible Tour Boat Captain: "Folks, straight ahead you can see the dam itself. If you look directly in front of us, you can see the mighty turbines that —"

Irresponsible Tour Boat Captain: "Hold on, son. You can't turn the wheel that hard."

Irresponsible Tour Boat Captain: "Ma'am. Can you get your son away from the wheel? I can't seem to pry his hands loose."

Irresponsible Tour Boat Captain: "Wow. He's got some grip."

Irresponsible Tour Boat Captain: "We're going the wrong way."

Irresponsible Tour Boat Captain: "I think he wet himself."

12

ARSENIC AND OLD LADIES

It took a year of living in California for my mother to decide that doctors were going to kill us all. I'm pretty sure that like Snow White, it all started with a poisoned piece of fruit.

The women in my family all lived into their nineties, and some even over a hundred. They held up pretty well too: able to walk, talk, complain, harass, underappreciate, and deride the self esteem of others right up to their last moments on earth. The men in my family all died younger than sixty, probably from being walked on, talked down to, complained about, harassed, underappreciated, and having their self esteem derided. Or it could have been the careless disregard they had for their own safety, like when my Great-Uncle Mike skateboarded down the side of a mountain, flipped over the guardrail, and plummeted to his doom. Also in California. That place is a death trap.

From the stories I was told about the formidable women of my clan, I never would have guessed they would have made it out of their thirties:

Mom: "My grandmother? Five foot nothing, three hundred pounds, smoked two packs a day. Ate everything covered in chicken fat."

Me: "So how old was she when she died?"

Mom: "Ninety two."

Me: "And her husband?"

Mom: "Fifty eight. He fell off the roof trying to clean the gutters during an ice storm."

Me: "Of course he did."

Mom: "SSSSStace. It was his time to go."

Me: "Of course it was."

Knowing this, I avoid things like skateboarding and gutter cleaning, but I wonder if there was more to it, some regimen these women followed that explained their longevity.

In 1979, we were driving from our house in New Jersey to visit my Great-Uncle Julius and Great-Aunt Toby, who lived in Palm Coast, Florida. It was about a fifteen hour drive. On the journey was me, my brother Layne the Favorite, my Aunt Adele, Mom, and my Grandma.

We had barely been on the road for an hour when the trouble started.

Aunt Adele: "I'm hungry."

Aunt Adele: "Carol. Are you hearing me? I'm hungry."

Mom: "What?"

Aunt Adele: "I'm hungry, I said."

Mom: "We just ate." Which was true. My mother had barbecued unspeakably black, crispy pancakes for breakfast that her mother, sister and son crunched their way through. I begged off.

Mom: "SSSStace. Why won't you eat my pancakes?"

Me: "They're burnt black."

Mom: "You know why? Because I don't use any butter in the pan. It's grease. It clogs your arteries. It's disgusting." Crunch, crunch, crunch.

Me: "I'm not hungry."

Mom: "What is *wrong* with you? These are made from barley. No disgusting white flour. Your brother likes them."

Layne the Favorite (grinning and nodding at me with ash-blackened barley teeth): "They're the best pancakes I ever had."

Mom: "Adele. It's ten thirty. You wanna stop for lunch?"

Aunt Adele: "It doesn't have to be anything big. Just a piece of fruit."

Me: "What?"

Aunt Adele: "Fruit! A piece of fruit!"

Grandma: "A piece of fruit would be good."

Mom: "You're right. We need a piece of fruit."

Aunt Adele: "That's what I've been saying! Just a piece of fruit!"

We drove in silence for ten miles while I tried to imagine what kind of outpost we could find that would stock pieces of fruit, as if on the side of the road there were big shirtless men with machetes who would hack up melons or grapefruits and sell travelers chunks of it. This happened for Teddy Roosevelt when he went on African safari in 1909 after leaving the White House. In 1979, alongside Interstate 95, it seemed ludicrous. Today, you can go to a McDonald's and get a piece of fruit. The women in my family were visionaries.

***

CIRCA 1980, TED the Drug Dealer's parents lived in the Lawrence Welk Retirement Village in Escondido, California. They owned a double-wide mobile home (a palace!) on top of a mountain. For me it was a pre-view of the bright aisles of Heaven: sunny all the time, big homes with no wheels, and everyone drove everywhere in golf carts. Because there was no age requirement, I got to scoot around in one whenever Layne the Favorite got tired of driving it.

The journey to Escondido wended through country roads lined with farmer's stands. My mother was delighted. She made Ted the Drug Dealer pull over at every one. The first time we went to visit his parents we didn't get there until nightfall. The back of our van was filled with citrus, lettuce, cabbages, tomatoes, cantaloupes, strawberries, potatoes, cucumbers, and at least a hundred red onions.

My mother had finally found a place where she could get a piece of fruit. Right there on the side of the road.

Ted the Drug Dealer's Mom: "Make sure you wash those."

Mom: "Don't be ridiculous, Ethel —"

Ted the Drug Dealer's Mom: "Esther."

Mom: "That's what I said. Listen to me. You can't wash fruit and vegetables. It takes away all the nutrientsssssssss."

Ted the Drug Dealer's Mom: "They treat those with poison to kill bugs."

Mom: "You know what's poison, Eleanor? Red meat. White bread." She shuddered. "Gravy. This is all-natural. Right from the ground. Natural."

Ted the Drug Dealer's Mom: "Esther."

Mom: "That's what I said. I don't think you're listening to me."

The insecticide used at the time was arsenic. This is how it killed the marauding bugs that attacked fruits and vegetables:

1. Confusion
2. Loss of motor control
3. Headaches
4. Hair loss
5. Severe diarrhea
6. Drowsiness
7. Muscle cramps
8. Convulsions
9. Night blindness

In 1980 California, you had to wash your fruits and vegetables with soap and water before eating them. You do not mess around with night blindness.

***

MY MOTHER DISHED up huge bowls of salad every single day. Unwashed piles of lettuce, cucumbers, spinach, radishes, and joyous handfuls of red onions, all crawling with latent death. We declined.

Mom: "Why aren't you eating my salad?" Crunch, crunch, crunch.

Layne the Favorite: "It tastes funny."

My mother looked at him, disappointment welling up in her face. He nervously twirled his fingers through his hair. A small clump of it fell out on to the table top.

Mom: "It tastes like nutrientsssssss." Crunch, crunch, crunch. "It's all-natural."

Layne the Favorite: "I'm having trouble seeing at night."

Mom: "Layner. It's night. It's dark. Of course you're having trouble seeing. What's *wrong* with you?"

Layne the Favorite looked horrified.

Me (waving): "I'm over here, Mom."

Mom: "Oh, right." Crunch, crunch, crunch.

Confusion. The first symptom of arsenic poisoning.

It didn't take long for my mother to zero in on her favorite farmer's market in Escondido - a huge complex of wooden stands covered in produce fresh from the acres of ground only a few yards away. The patriarch of the farming family was a lean, weathered man named Roger. I'm fairly certain he founded the Whole Foods chain of natural food stores a few years later.

Mom (crunching on a pear she had picked up from the stand): "Rufus. What's good today?"

Roger: "Carol. You can't eat that."

My mother stumbled and nearly fell. Roger had to catch her and prop her up. Loss of motor control. The second symptom of arsenic poisoning.

Mom: "Robert. Ted will pay for it."

Roger: "I mean you have to wash it first."

Mom: "That's crazy, Roland. That washes off all the nutrients."

Roger: "Carol, we spray all our produce with arsenic. You have to wash everything."

Mom: "I can't listen to your *chazerai* right now, Richard. My head is killing me."

Third symptom.

A week later, Roger escalated his argument. Huge hand-lettered signs were arranged strategically around his produce stand:

DO <u>NOT</u> EAT UNWASHED PRODUCE

My mother glared at the signs.

Mom: "Rudy! Rudy!" She stalked over to him, staggering slightly. Some bright red hairs were lifted from her head and carried away by the breeze. "What is all this? It's disgusting."

Roger (patiently): "Carol. My produce is straight from the ground. It has to be cleaned before you eat it."

Mom: "Well. Raymond. I never heard of this. What kind of farmer are you?"

She plucked a strawberry and chomped on it.

Mom: "Ted will pay for that."

The next week, Roger tried another tactic: he set up fruit and vegetable washing stands: spray bottles of fresh water and dish detergent.

Roger: "Carol. How about you wash that nectarine?"

Mom: "No way! Not on your life, Reggie. Disgusting. You make me sick." Chomp.

Since that was essentially true, Roger had no reply.

Near the end of the season, my mother got herself banned from her favorite produce stand.

Mom: "Look, Layner. Ronnie's waiting for me. I'm his favorite customer! I told you."

Me: "He looks unhappy."

Roger: "Carol. You can't buy anything here anymore. You have to get yourself to a doctor."

My mother's eyes widened and her cheek twitched. It was likely a muscle cramp - symptom number seven.

Mom: "Rupert. What are you talking about?"

Roger: "I'm not selling you any more produce. You have to buy your fruit at Ralph's from now on. They wash it for you. That's safest."

Mom: "Ralph? Who the hell is Ralph? What are you talking about?"

Roger: "Ralph's grocery store. They're everywhere."

Mom: "Rudy. There's no way. No way! You know what happens when you wash fruit? The nutrients disappear. The nutrientsssssss!"

Roger folded his arms. Ted the Drug Dealer led my mother away, back to the van. She slept all the way home, even though she had just woken up an hour before.

Drowsiness: symptom number six.

Ted the Drug Dealer took my mother to a doctor. A simple hair follicle test confirmed what Roger the farsighted farmer already knew. We were told that night at dinner. The giant salad bowl sat empty in the middle of the table.

Mom: "Layner. This is going to be hard for you to hear. Apparently Mommy's sick."

Layne the Favorite: "What's wrong?"

Mom: "That quack thinks I have the arsenic poisoning."

Ted the Drug Dealer: "You do, Carol. He showed me the test results. Your arsenic levels were so high they didn't fit on the printout."

Mom: "Quack. Doctors will kill us all."

She abandoned the quack's treatment and found a holistic healer in San Diego who put her on a regimen of expensive drops he mixed himself in his shop. By the time we moved to Lake Tahoe six months later, her arsenic levels were nearly normal.

Mom (triumphantly): "See that? Doctors don't know anything. I've been buying fresh fruit and vegetables from a produce stand that *wantssss* my business and I haven't been washing off the stinkin' nutrientssss and I'm fine."

We had been secretly washing her produce, which turned out to be a huge mistake.

We spent the next seven years (classic Old Testament punishment time) with no remedies for anything – no pain killers, aspirin, hemorrhoid cream (apparently Ted the Drug Dealer had some difficulties from driving a cab all day) or antibiotics. I once had an untreated ear infection so bad that I couldn't hear out of one ear for a month.

Until she married Marvin, King of the Jews, my mother followed the tenets of a succession of holistic healers:

1. Antibiotics destroy your body's natural defenses
2. Aspirin shreds your intestines
3. White flour is evil
4. Painkillers mask symptoms
5. Red meat is evil
6. Never wash the fruit. Ever.

I left for college in 1988. My mother started dating Marvin, King of the Jews shortly thereafter. I came home for winter break and was required to have dinner with Mom and her new boyfriend. I made every excuse I could think of, but there was no way out.

My mother put food on the table. London broil, mashed potatoes, fresh green beans covered in real butter. The salad had no red onions on it. There was a bowl of gravy. I suddenly felt like I had the first four symptoms of arsenic poisoning.

Me: "Mom! What the hell happened?"

Marvin, King of the Jews: "Don't talk to your mutha like that."

Mom: "SSSSSSStace. What are you talking about?"

Me: "Red meat. White potatoes. Butter. God help us all - gravy?"

Marvin, King of the Jews: "What is *wrong* with you?"

Great. Now there were two of them.

13

ELECTROCUTION AND LOST CATS

OUR WINNEBAGO LIMPED its way into San Diego a month after we left New Jersey. By then, I'd had enough of trailer trash living. There were plenty of reasons why:

1. Near-death mishaps like the one at Hoover Dam.
2. The motor home broke down every other day in the American Southwest at the hottest time of the year.
3. We had a bathroom no bigger than the trunk of a compact car.
4. My family was at closer proximity than anyone really needed.
5. In San Diego I discovered two more reasons:
6. I was not allowed to have a pet.
7. The camper, along with its many other engineering failures, had become electrified.

Well. That didn't take long.

***

IT SHOULDN'T HAVE been a surprise that we couldn't have pets in the motor home. Before we left New Jersey, Ted the Lightbulb Salesman insisted that we give away Lassie, a giant collie we'd had for as long as I could remember.

Ted the Lightbulb Salesman: "The camper is too small to have that dog in it. It weighs eighty pounds!"

Layne the Favorite (not for the first time): "She's a she, not an it." Lassie was his dog, which he reminded me at every opportunity.

Me: "*I* weigh eighty pounds."

Mom: "SSSSStace. Hush. We know."

Great. So it was me or the dog. I couldn't wait to see how this turned out.

* * *

Jews love trips.

It's all in the Old Testament: exile from the Garden of Eden, forty days and forty nights on Noah's cruise ship, Joseph bringing his whole family to eventual slavery in Egypt, Moses wandering the desert, and the Diaspora.

We Jews, as a people, need a better travel agent.

My mother and Ted the Lightbulb Salesman had the same nomadic spirit as our ancestors. Three thousand years after the early Israelites packed up their goats, donned their orthotic sandals, and headed out into the desert with no destination or water, my parents planned our exodus from New Jersey. I could only hope they were not trusting the same Guy who had commanded Abraham to sacrifice his only son, or David to face down a giant Philistine with nothing but a slingshot to get us to the promised land.

Everything that we owned was divided into two piles: *Going or Staying.*

This would not be the first time that size mattered: it was either small enough to fit in the Winnebago or the trailer we were towing behind it, or it was left behind.

The dog didn't make it.

✳ ✳ ✳

To THIS DAY, Ted the Drug Dealer can count on one hand the number of battles he won against Layne the Favorite. Most of them happened early in his marriage to my mother, when she could still be persuaded by the argument, "But I'm your *husband.*" It quit working around the time Ted the Lightbulb Salesman ran our only car off a cliff in Northern California a year later.

Well. That didn't take long.

My mother had found a family a few blocks away who was willing to take Lassie off our hands. In classic 1970's parenting style, Layne the Favorite and I knew nothing about these arrangements until the Saturday in June when we were told to walk the dog over to her new foster home and give her away.

In retrospect, we were lucky that Ted the Lightbulb Salesman, in later years, a legendary slayer of dogs, didn't just shoot her in the head and hand us a shovel.

✳ ✳ ✳

THE PATERSONS WERE a great family - two daughters in their teens, a mother who stayed home all the time, and the same father who had been there from the beginning. Their house was gigantic, and its back yard had actual grass instead of a paved over place for extra parking.

Mrs. Paterson had baked for us.

I looked around their first floor, munching a warm cookie, while the dog scampered around with the two girls.

Me: "What's your basement like?"

I asked that question about every new house I went into. When my mother turned the first floor of our house into a beauty salon, she rented out the second floor to a serial killer and we moved into the unfinished basement. I slept on a fold out couch with my brother. I believed that everyone lived the way I did, so I assumed the Patersons, despite their plushly appointed bedrooms, trooped down to their basement to sleep when it got dark.

Mrs. Paterson: "Um...it's a finished basement. Carpeted. The laundry room's down there." She looked helplessly at my brother, who was glaring at his traitorous dog as she wagged her tail and grinned like a fool at her new people.

Me: "Carpet. Snazzy. Sleeper sofa, or sleeping bags?"

Mrs. Paterson: "I'm not sure what you're asking."

Me: "Never mind. Layne. Let's go."

I was in a hurry to get back home and suggest to my parents that they take the dog with them and leave me with the Patersons, their carpeted basement, and a real back yard. They looked like the kind of fine, upstanding people who could be persuaded to get a pool. Also, Mrs. Paterson could cook.

I was sure that Layne the Favorite would be onboard with my plan. I took another cookie for the road - if I packed on more weight I'd be over the limit for motor home travel. I imagined waving my pudgy hand from the Paterson's front porch as my mother, Ted the Lightbulb Salesman, Layne the Favorite, and his dog drove away in the Winnebago.

I would wait until nightfall of the first day before suggesting a pool to the Patersons, to better ease them into the idea.

***

TRAILER PARKS ARE full of stray animals. Most of us cooked outside on grills, so there were always scraps of food lying around. When people left this trailer park for the next one, many of them left their pets behind. Something to do with a weight limit. Like our Biblical ancestors, we were nomads; if our animals couldn't provide meat or milk or were too heavy to transport, they got left behind.

That didn't stop me from befriending Shmutz, a small brown tabby who showed up one day mewling and peeping outside the Winnebago.

Ted the Lightbulb Salesman had been transferred to San Diego by his company and still went to work every day in a full suit and tie. The other trailer park folk stared as he passed by them looking like the Queen's butler. He avoided the cat carefully, not wanting to get any Shmutz on his suit.

Ted the Lightbulb Salesman: "Whatever you do, do NOT feed that cat."

I waited until he was gone before bolting inside the Winnebago for tuna and milk. The Twelfth Commandment (honor thy mother and father), was vague about stepfathers. Until the rabbis took one side or the other, I'd make my own rules regarding Ted the Lightbulb

Salesman's orders. My only concession in respect to Biblical tradition was waiting until he was gone.

Shmutz plowed his way through a can of tuna and a bowl of milk while I briefed him on the house rules:

1. Don't eat my mother's cooking unless you like red onions and whatever sorrow tastes like.
2. Avoid Ted the Lightbulb Salesman. Pets are not his thing. Trust me on this.
3. Eat slower. If you gain too much weight, we'll have to leave you behind.

The cat was eating so fast that his head bobbed up and down as if he was nodding. Smart cat.

✳✳✳

LAYNE THE FAVORITE: "That stupid cat's back again."

We were coming back from the pool. Most trailer parks could be counted on to have a centralized body of water of some kind. The one in Imperial Beach not only had a huge pool, but it was located next to Coronado Bay.

Every trailer used some kind of bottled gas for cooking and we sat oblivious atop our own sewage, which was kept in flimsy plastic tanks. We could expect Armageddon when some chain smoker flipped a lit butt at a leaky propane tank. The gas would explode, ignite our stored shit, and the ragged survivors would flee for the water as our mobile homes burned flat behind us.

Shmutz the Cat, unaware of our impending demise, sat on the concrete pad where the Winnebago was parked. He was in the spot where I always put his food, but only he and I knew that.

Layne the Favorite swept past Shmutz, ignoring the cat's happy peeping. He grabbed the camper's heavy metal doorknob (it was actually more like the lever on a walk-in freezer), bent over suddenly, made a choked gurgling sound, and fell to the ground. His own urine puddled under him.

Me: "What happened?"

Layne the Favorite: "I got shocked!"

Me: "No way!"

I stepped forward and grabbed the lever, yanking the door open. Electricity coursed through me. I felt all my muscles clench as my bladder let go. I sat down heavily on the ground next to my brother. Our bodies trembled uncontrollably. We did not smell good.

We stared at the open doorway of the camper. It was metal, as was the door and the fold-down step we used to get in. In fact, just about every available surface was metal, and we were soaking wet. Shmutz the Cat walked over, sniffed at us, and peed on the ground.

Layne the Favorite: "How will we get in?"

Me: "Get in? How many times does this thing have to try and kill us before we learn our lesson? I think we should go back to the pool and wait for Mom to get home."

Layne the Favorite: "And just leave the door open?"

Me: "I really don't think anyone will go in there."

Shmutz the Cat, seeing an opportunity, streaked for the open camper. His wet feet touched the metal step. His fur spiked and he shrieked. He bolted away, a mad, spiky puffball.

Layne the Favorite: "Stupid cat."

***

WE STUDIED THE problem: the open door, the metal step, the steel door-frame, the unseen menace of electricity coursing through every available surface, and our sodden state.

Me: "Maybe if we don't touch the ground and the camper at the same time we won't get shocked."

Layne the Favorite: "That's stupid. Can you levitate?"

Me: "Excellent! Back to the pool then!"

Layne the Favorite: "All right. Try it."

I got up off the ground, reeking of pee, steadied myself, and ran at full speed for the door. I leaped at the last minute and landed on the metal step with both feet. Bolts of electricity thundered up my legs. My whole body contorted. I bit my tongue. My legs buckled and I fell to the concrete, blood and drool pouring from my mouth.

Me: "Dint work. Oo try ith."

***

LAYNE THE FAVORITE and I were sitting outside on the ground when Ted the Lightbulb Salesman got home. He stepped out of the car in his immaculate suit, his shined shoes crunching on the gravel as he approached.

Ted the Lightbulb Salesman: "Why are you sitting out here? What's that smell?"

Me: "The camper's electrified."

Ted the Lightbulb Salesman: "No it's not."

He stalked to the open door and put his hand on the metal door-frame, meaning to step up and inside. He cramped up and spun halfway around, his face crumpling, his hand glued to the doorframe. His left eye twitched. He pissed himself and staggered away from the camper. He tried to catch himself on the picnic table and missed, shredding his suit pants as he fell to the ground. He lay on his back on the concrete, staring blankly upward, his tie half across his face.

Ted the Lightbulb Salesman: "Son of a bitch!"

Layne the Favorite: "Told you."

Ted the Lightbulb Salesman lay there for a few minutes, breathing heavily. I figured electricity was kind of his area: he had to know something about it in order to sell lightbulbs all day long. He got up suddenly, like he always did when his purpose was clear, and stomped around to the back of the camper. His right hand brushed the aluminum ladder that led to the roof. I saw a spark.

Ted the Lightbulb Salesman: "Shit!"

He unplugged the thick cord that connected the Winnebago to the power. We were saved.

***

WE ATE DINNER outside that night while waiting for the motor home repairman to come and see why, not for the first time, our home had become a death trap. My mother was in a state of high disgust. She went inside and hauled everything perishable out of the fridge and plunked it down on the picnic table: a green salad crawling with onions and latent death (she had not yet learned to wash the arsenic off the vegetables), a pot of chicken soup, bones poking out of its surface like tree limbs in a dank swamp, and yesterday's liver. She opened cans of green beans and sloshed them into a bowl.

Mom: "Dinner. Dissssssssgusting."

Me: "The soup's cold. And has bones in it."

Mom: "SSSSStace. How am I gonna heat it up? And you love my chicken soup!"

Me: "It tastes like fatigue. And the gas still works."

Mom: "Oh right." Her memory was slipping; it was all the arsenic she was ingesting. "I'll heat it up. Then you'll eat it, Buster."

Me: "Has anyone seen that brown cat that's been hanging around?"

Ted the Lightbulb Salesman stared at me, struggling to chew yesterday's cold, rubbery liver.

Ted the Lightbulb Salesman: "Have you been feeding it?"

Me: "Ted. Seriously. You think giving it our food would make it want to stay?"

Ted the Lightbulb Salesman: "It's probably dead."

Me: "Dead? Really? Isn't it possible it found someplace else to spend its time?"

My mother brought out a plastic container of mashed potatoes coated in onions and minced garlic. It tasted like the feet sweat of men who dwelled in purgatory.

Mom: "Probably got hung up in some bushes and starved to death."

Me: "Couldn't it have gotten hit by a car or eaten by a shark? Something quick?"

Ted the Lightbulb Salesman: "I think your mother's right. But it would die of thirst long before it starved to death."

Me: "Oh my God!"

Mom: "SSSSSSSStace. Listen. When it's your time to go, it's your time to go."

I spent the next several days scouring the trailer park for any sign of Shmutz. I sliced myself to ribbons crawling through hedges. There was no trace of him. I like to think he found a new family with better food and a home that didn't fry him when he tried to go inside. I wished I could have gone with him.

I had really had it with trailer life. Only four and a half years to go...

14

TRAILER PARK SPORTS

I GOT HIT by a car in 1983 because you can't play baseball in a trailer park.

My brother Layne the Favorite and I didn't play much baseball after we moved into a Winnebago and left New Jersey, where we had friends and a back yard to play in. He had also lost some of his enthusiasm for playing with me since I turned out to be a better pitcher than he was. I kept reminding him that he had many other fine qualities, not the least of which was that Mom always liked him best.

He finally relented when we lived in Florida, after a long loop around the country. We went out in the trailer park's street, next to the bar where we had once taken our mother's special cache of silver certificate five-dollar bills and spent them on video games.

Mom: "I can't believe you took those five dollar bills! They were an invessssstment! And to talk your brother into this! You know he's too nice to be a criminal!"

Me: "He sure enjoyed hitting high score on Centipede while being underage in a bar."

Mom: "SSSSStace. What is *wrong* with you? You stole money. Do you get that?"

Me: "Maybe you should have hid them better. And the lock on that cash box you left in the storage compartment next to the sewage tank under the rusty pipes behind the spare propane canisters was pretty flimsy. You'd think it would take more than a couple hits with a big rock to bust it open."

Mom: "That was your brother's college fund!"

Me: "Fine. He can have mine, then."

My mother stared at me blankly. I surmised that perhaps I didn't have a college fund. Hard to believe. Better to just wait a few years to find out for sure.

Mom: "You're just like your father, that son of a bitch."

I doubted that. There was no way Dad could beat my score on Pac Man; he was color blind and had carpal tunnel syndrome. I would have smoked him. Unless she meant the thing about the money - after I was born he took all the cash I got from my circumcision to the track and lost it betting on a gelding named Snippet while I was still simmering in my incubator. Isn't that a kick in the recently bobbed genitalia?

$$***$$

HERE'S HOW YOU know there are a lot of large windows in a trailer park:

1. Look around. Each trailer has a huge back window. The ones you can drive have huge front windows, too.

2. Toss a baseball back and forth for about five minutes. You'll see angry faces start to pop up in the windows.
3. If you're out there long enough the trailer park manager (or his representative), will come along on his speedy golf cart and say something indicative.

Trailer Park Manager (or his representative): "What the hell are you doing?"

Me (shrugging eloquently): "Playing baseball."

Trailer Park Manager (or his representative): "So you're some kind of smart ass."

Me: "Recent polls have me pegged as a son of a bitch. And a criminal. And a corrupter of the innocent." I jerked my chin at Layne the Favorite. "Him."

Trailer Park Manager (or his representative): "Didn't I see you two coming out of the bar the other day?"

Me: "Top score on Pac Man. Only cost sixty bucks."

Trailer Park Manager (or his representative): "Quit playing ball in the street. Can't you see all the windows?"

***

WE TOOK OUR dilemma to Ted the Drug Dealer. When it came to defiance of authority, he was our spirit guide. His nuanced interpretation of interactions with those in charge was worthy of the ancient philosophers.

Ted the Drug Dealer: "That's total bullshit. We pay rent here. You can shit right in the middle of the street if you want." I could almost picture him walking through the woods of ancient Greece with Socrates and Plato, the marbled city of Athens in the misty background.

Me: "Thanks, Ted. Good parenting. See you around." To Layne the Favorite: "Let's go."

Layne the Favorite: "I don't think we should. We almost got in trouble. Mom will be pretty mad at you if something happens."

Ted the Drug Dealer: "I'll go with you."

We were dumbfounded. Ted the Drug Dealer was going to play baseball? I sensed an actual father-son moment in the offing. Our first ever!

***

THE THREE OF us went out into the street of the trailer park. Lined up on both sides, glinting in the late afternoon sunlight, were rows of big windows. I tried to ignore them. Ted the Drug Dealer stood in the middle of the street. Layne the Favorite stood opposite him and a few dozen feet away.

Layne the Favorite: "Me first!"

I shrugged and sat down on a nearby picnic table to watch, listening for the sound of the trailer park manager's (or his representative's) golf cart.

Kids - don't try this at home. Oh, wait. If your home isn't on wheels and you don't live in a trailer park, it might actually turn out okay for you. Go ahead - try it at home.

Ted the Drug Dealer was Ted the Cab Driver then, so he was dressed in saggy blue jeans, a short sleeve button down shirt with a pocket on each breast. These pockets were overflowing with business cards from people he picked up, parking stubs, gas receipts, and pens. On his belt was a wallet on a chain, a huge keychain full of keys, his holstered .22 pistol, a bowie knife, and a blackjack. His pants pockets were full of coins. He creaked and jingled with every step.

He looked around for any signs of authority, smirked, and threw the ball, a bent elbow, hand by ear, looping arm motion that we referred to as *throwing like a girl*. The ball sailed high in the air and crashed through the huge back window of the trailer whose picnic table I was sitting on. Glass rained down. Through the now open window, I heard, "Son of a bitch!"

Layne the Favorite's eyes widened. He bolted past me and into our Winnebago, followed closely by a frantically jingling Ted the Drug Dealer, who left a silver trail of bright coins in his high stepping wake. Almost simultaneously, I heard the metallic slam of the Winnebago's door and the electric whine of the trailer park manager's golf cart. He had not sent his representative.

Trailer Park Manager: "Well, well, well."

Me: "Oh boy."

***

I WAS A great disappointment to my mother that day.

Mom: "SSSSSSSStace. I can't believe you did that."

Me: "Neither can I."

Layne the Favorite and Ted the Drug Dealer had each discovered some pressing business far, far away from our motor home that night. Ted the Drug Dealer was shopping for one of those belt mounted coin dispensers so he could better organize his loose change. Running to the

Winnebago had cost him nearly three bucks. Layne the Favorite said he was going along to buy a present for his mother, who looked so sad about the events of the day.

Mom: "Layner. You're such a good boy."

***

I HIT UPON a solution pretty quickly, but needed co-conspirators.

Me: "Hey, Ted. How about a ride to the mall?

Ted the Drug Dealer: "No. Besides, you can't afford the fare."

Me: "Fare? I think we're way past the fare, my friend. I'm sure my mother would be very interested to hear what really happened to that window."

He leaned forward in his seat. Some business cards fell out of his pocket. He grimaced as his new coin changer dug into his belly. Its mechanism ratcheted and fifty cents fell on the floor.

Ted the Drug Dealer: "You think she'll believe it wasn't you?"

He had me there. Well played, Ted.

***

I RODE MY bike to the Hollywood Mall, which was only two miles away. I found what I wanted at Sears: a whiffle ball and bat. No chance of breaking any windows with that.

On my way back, I was stopped at the light where Pembroke Road crossed 20th street. I could see the beer signs in the bar that let me know I was near home. The light turned green and I started through the crosswalk to the concrete median strip that bisected the four-lane road.

A huge black Cadillac moved from a dead stop and started a sweeping left turn. I could see only a small tuft of hair and the top rim of huge eyeglasses above the steering wheel. I hit the grille and rolled up onto the hood. My face pressed against the driver's side windshield and I stared down into the lined, ancient face of the driver. Mrs. Lindbergh stared straight ahead and kept driving, grimacing at the screeching sound my bike made as it was crushed under the wheels. Flying on instruments, she didn't seem to notice the boy pressed up against her window.

By the way, my head didn't break the window. Not even a crack. To this day, I have yet to break a window. It's all in the Mother's Day card I'm sending this year.

A plumber in a pickup truck who had been stopped at the red light gunned his engine, ran the light, and cut Mrs. Lindbergh off. When she stopped, I rolled off the hood and landed in the median strip, where I sat quietly, checking for damage. Pants ripped, shirt torn, one shoe missing. My bike (and my whiffle ball equipment) was nowhere to be found.

The plumber called the cops. There had actually been a patrol car at the trailer park bar, breaking up a fight between two of the patrons over whose turn it was on the Pac Man machine. The cops left their car and walked out to the median strip. They made Mrs. Lindbergh get out of her Cadillac.

Mrs. Lindbergh: "Look, Buster. I don't know what this *facochten chazerai* is, you *momser*."

Patrolman 1: "Ma'am, I have no idea what you just said."

Me (wearily): "She doesn't know what this fucking bullshit is, you bastard."

Patrolman 1 (dangerously): "You better watch your mouth, boy."

Me: "I was translating. I speak Old Crabby Bitch."

Patrolman 1: "Ah."

Mrs. Lindbergh: "I don't know why you're hauling me out of my car, Buster. I'll have your *schvants* in a *zwinge, shlemiel.*"

Patrolman 1 looked at me expectantly.

Me: "Your dick in a vise, jackass."

Patrolman 1: "Thanks, son."

Me: "Belt her with your nightstick and cuff her right quick if you want to retain the proper use of your goodies, Officer."

Patrolman 1: "Ma'am, are you aware that you hit this boy with your car?"

Mrs. Lindbergh: "What? What boy?"

Patrolman 1 pointed at me. I waved. She glared at me through her bottle-glass spectacles.

Mrs. Lindbergh: "No way! I most certainly did not hit any *facochten mazik.*"

Me (to Patrolman 1): "Fucking little devil."

Patrolman 1: "Wow. That's pretty mean."

Me: "Not when you consider that she hit me with her *facochten* Cadillac."

Patrolman 1: "That's a good one, son."

Mrs. Lindbergh: "I didn't hit anyone with my car! This is total *shmontses*."

Me: "Another word for bullshit."

Mrs. Lindbergh glared at me.

Mrs. Lindbergh: "*Halts moyl, leman a-shem,* you *tahkshit. Ikh feif af dir.*"

Me: "Shut up, for God's sake, you brat. You should go to hell."

Patrolman 1 (marveling): "Wow. Nasty."

I looked at Mrs. Lindbergh.

Me: "*Gay kaken afen yan,* you *klafteh.*"

Mrs. Lindbergh's breath stopped. Her eyes widened and she fell back a step against her car. Her mouth trembling, she grabbed Patrolman 1's arm. He helped her sit back down in the driver's seat of her car. He looked at me.

Me: "I told the old bitch to go shit in the ocean."

Patrolman 1 grinned. "Nice."

***

PATROLMAN 1 LEFT his partner to handle the citation for Mrs. Lindbergh, who was squawking for *mit avocat* (her lawyer). The cops had dragged the wreckage of my bike and my flattened whiffle ball and bat from under the Cadillac. Patrolman 1 helped me wheel my bike back to the Winnebago. The trailer park manager, who had been presiding over the nearby bar fight, zoomed over in his golf cart.

Trailer Park Manager: "What'd he do now, Officer?"

Patrolman 1: "Some woman ran him over with her car."

Trailer Park Manager: "I can see that. He's got a mouth on him."

Patrolman 1 (chuckling): "That he does."

Me: *"Ir kinder vet mir makhn an arbm-shvakh."*

Trailer Park Manager: "Fucking kid's speaking in tongues! Tase him!"

Me: "I said you kids are gonna give me a nervous breakdown."

Patrolman 1 looked at me quizzically. I shrugged.

Me: "I only know the things that have been said to me."

Patrolman 1: "That's some childhood you got there."

Me: "You don't know the half of it."

Patrolman 1: "By the way, kid. Doesn't everyone shit in the ocean? I mean, eventually?"

Me: "Jews don't like to be reminded of it. We've had to swim in it ever since we lost the ability to split it in two."

15

THE CHRISTMAS COOK-OFF

Rob's mother, Victoria, could cook better than anyone I knew. Trust me, I checked. All it took was a description of whatever hellish dish my mother had concocted for dinner the night before, and I could get anyone to cook for me. Their food, whatever it was, was always delicious.

However, Victoria was a magician with food. She could turn leftovers from three different meals into a banquet. Give her fresh ingredients and she could amaze and delight even the most diehard food snobs. But there was one day of the year when she pulled out all the stops, making the best food I had ever had.

That one day was Christmas, and I was her token Jew.

***

Victoria: "Roberto. Tell your pasty Jewish friend to come for Kreemas dinner."

I was eating a salami and provolone sandwich on a crusty roll. His mother had put a stack of them on a plate and left them for us when we got to his house after school. Rob took one bite and his face wrinkled.

Rob: "Mom. How old is this roll?"

Victoria: "Yesterday." Rob put the sandwich down. I grabbed it.

Rob: "Yesterday's roll? Really? And the salami is a little greasy."

Me: "Let me tell you about the last sandwich I had that my mother made. Chicken thighs coated in paprika, crunchy with cartilage. Fat free cheese and bitter lettuce. Soy mayonnaise. On bread made from turnip flour."

Rob: "Ugh. How many onion slices? No. Don't tell me."

Me: "Four. It tasted like something that grew in cemetery dirt."

Rob: "Take the fucking sandwiches."

Victoria: "Roberto!"

Rob: "You wanna come over for Christmas dinner? Not like you're doing anything."

My mouth was stuffed with bread, cheese and salami. I could only nod. Vigorously.

***

THAT DAY, FOR the first time in my life, I felt like a kid on Christmas morning. Everyone noticed.

Mom: "Why are you so happy?"

Me: "Because I won't be home for dinner."

Layne the Favorite: "That's a mean thing to say to my mother. Where are you going?"

Me: "Rob's house."

Mom: "What's she making?" My mother always asked this question - she had to know what was on other people's menus, as if she was some kind of domestic food critic.

Me: "Lasagna. Black beans and rice. Meatballs as big as a baby's head. Sausage —"

Mom (horrified): "Sausage?"

Me (dreamily): "Yesssssss."

Mom: "SSSSStace! That has pork in it! Pork!"

Me: "Good lord, Ma, *everything* will have pork in it. The lasagna, the beans, the meatballs. Everything." I may have drooled a little.

Mom: "SSSStace. None of that sounds kosher."

Me: "None of it is. And I know what I'm talking about; I went to Hebrew school."

Mom: "Lotta good that did. Cost me three thousand buckssss a year. Look outside. Do you see a tree out there, SSSSSStace? Do I have a tree?"

I looked outside. There were several trees.

Me: "There's a bunch of trees."

Mom (teeth gritted): "SSSSSStace. A tree! A tree!"

Layne the Favorite: "She means a money tree."

Mom: "That's what I said. You know what I could have bought with three thousand bucks a year?"

Me: "Another Winnebago?"

Mom: "A Winnebago? What is *wrong* with you? All I got for my money was a pork eating, ungrateful son."

She got up and stomped over to the phone. She put on her half-glasses, got out her address book, and started dialing.

Me: "Who are you calling?" She ignored me.

Mom (into the phone): "Dinner!"

Mom: "What do you mean, 'Who is this?' Vivian. It's Carol. Yes. That's what I said. SSSSSo. I undersssssstand that my son is having dinner at your house?"

She paused, her finger jabbing straight up in the air, her lips thin, her teeth gritted. I winced. My Christmas miracle was ruined.

Her hand fell to her side. Her jaw unclenched, and she smiled. I was saved.

Mom: "Viola. That is so sweet. We'd love to come."

Me: "Noooooooooooooooo!"

Mom: "That's what I said. We're on our way now. I can help you cook."

She hung up the phone and beamed at me.

Me: "I'll stay here."

Mom: "Oh no you won't, Buster."

***

THE WORST THING about the drive over was that we made all the green lights; the car never slowed down enough for me to leap out and save myself. Plus, I was stuffed in the backseat with the essential components of my mother's gear. These were the staples she took with her anytime she cooked at someone else's house:

1. A ten-pound bag of red onions
2. A mesh sack of whole garlic cloves
3. An industrial sized can of paprika
4. A cooler with two kosher chickens
5. The contents of Satan's spice cabinet.

I tried to reason with her:

Me: "Ma. You know they probably have all the food they need. I don't think we need to carry all this stuff inside."

Mom: "Where did you say his mother's from? Denmark?"

Me: "The Dominican Republic."

Mom: "That's what I said. She doesn't know how to cook kosher."

Me: "She's not *trying* to cook kosher!"

Mom: "So what are we gonna eat? She knows we're Jewisssssssh!"

Me: "You weren't invited!"

Mom: "What are you talking about? Of course we were invited. I talked to her on the phone this morning."

Me: "And I'm sure she has enough onions."

Mom: "No one does, Buster."

I looked out the window at the scenery speeding by. I was going to jump out. It would mean a few weeks in the hospital, but it would be worth it. Mmmm. Hospital food.

But it was too late. We had arrived.

***

ROB AND HIS mother came out of the house as soon as we pulled up. I staggered out of the car, the cooler in one hand, the bags of hideous vegetables and spices in the other. Rob looked at me mournfully.

Me: "Run. Save yourself."

Victoria approached and gave my mother a hug. She smelled like stewed tomatoes, spicy sausage, and freshly baked bread. My mother smelled like hair spray, overpowering citrus perfume, and peppermint gum.

Victoria: "Merry Kreemas."

Mom: "This is just another day to us, Fatima. We don't celebrate Christmasssss. We're Jewisssssh."

Victoria: "Victoria."

Mom: "That's what I said. I brought onions."

Victoria: "Onions? Is dat a Jewish tradition?"

Me: "It's her tradition. A religion all her own."

The two women looked at me.

Mom: "I never know what's wrong with him. He's just like his father. Have you met my son? This is Layne. Isn't he handsome? And such a good boy. Not a smart aleck like the other one."

Victoria: "Si. He's a preence."

Mom: "A what? SSSSStace. Her accent doesn't sound Danish. What did she say?"

Me: "She said he's a prince."

She stared at Victoria for a moment. We went inside.

* * *

I WAS ORDERED to put the travel kit in the kitchen. I stood in front of the stove, gazing in wonder at the scene before me. I felt like falling to my knees in worshipful awe.

1. Fresh baked, crusty bread cooling on the counter.
2. Two lasagnas covered with molten cheese in the oven.
3. A bubbling pot on the stove filled to the brim with black beans and rice.
4. Another pot with meatballs simmering in Victoria's homemade tomato sauce.
5. A pan with seared Italian sausage on the front burner.

6. A platter of prosciutto ham, sliced tomatoes, and fresh mozzarella, coated in basil, oregano and cilantro.
7. A giant salad bowl of fresh greens, red cabbage, carrots, cucumbers, black and green olives next to a cruet of homemade Italian dressing.

My mother sniffed from behind me.

Mom: "Disssgusting. All that pork."

Me: "Merry Christmas!"

Mom: "Give me that bag of onions."

I dropped the onions and fled.

✳ ✳ ✳

ROB AND I hovered at the edge of the kitchen entryway like nervous observers of a delicate surgery, or ringside managers of two prize fighters.

On one side was my skinny, redheaded mother, taller than average, wearing designer jeans and a flowery shirt, her fingers covered in rings, her long fingernails painted orange. She peered down her nose at her two small chickens in a pan, powdering them thickly with paprika. Whole, unpeeled garlic cloves were piled around them. She added more at random, then picked up the paprika can and sprinkled generously.

On the other side was Victoria, whose head only reached my mother's shoulder. She was built low and solid like a fireplug. Her hands moved like an orchestra conductor's as she pulled the lasagnas out of the oven at just the right time, sliced the bread, and lowered the heat on the beans and rice to a perfect simmer. She poked a meatball and studied the consistency of the sauce.

Victoria: "Carol, I have meenced garlic. You can rub eet into da skeen. Also butter to keep the skeen from drying out."

Mom: "Freida. Do you know what's in butter?"

Victoria: "Victoria. Milk, crem, and salt."

Mom: "Fat. Nothing but fat. And I like a crispy skin."

Victoria: "You could peel dat garlic an put half inside da birds."

Mom: "What about the other half, Vanessa?"

Victoria: "Trow them in da garbage. And eet's Victoria."

Mom: "Why do you keep telling me your name? Is that a Danish thing, or a Goyisher Christmas thing?"

* * *

WITHIN HALF AN hour my mother was into the onions. She was chopping them madly; the pile reached halfway to the ceiling. Red bits were scattered all over the counter and stuck to the walls. She had two cutting boards going. Victoria had been slugging down Dominican Mamajuana, a drink made from dark rum, red wine, and honey, valued for its calming powers. It must not have been working—both women were openly weeping. Victoria was weaving slightly. She picked chunks of onion out of my mother's hair.

Victoria: "Dat's a lot of onions. What they for, all dem onions?"

Mom: "I told you, Valerie. They're for the salad. How do you make a salad without onions? Maybe if you weren't such a heavy drinker you could remember what I'm telling you." She turned and glared at me.

Mom: "SSSStace. His mother's a drinker? I didn't know that."

Me: "I think she just started today."

Victoria gulped a nearly full glass of Mamajuana, tears running down her cheeks.

Victoria: "You gonna kill somebody wit da onions. And my name's Vivian."

Rob: "No it's not! It's Victoria!"

The women turned to stare at us, their eyes red and dripping. They spoke at the same time:

"That's what I said!"

***

WE SAT AROUND the huge table. One of the two lasagnas was placed proudly in the middle, next to my mother's shrunken paprika-garlic devil chickens. The top third of the salad bowl was red onions; my mother had scooped out some of the lettuce to make room and dropped it in the trash. Rob's mother defensively drank Mamajuana and cackled at the sight of it.

Victoria: "So much for da fuckin salad."

Mom: "Yasmine. It's better this way."

Victoria: "You won' be able to taste anyting except da onions, Carla."

Mom: "Carol. Why is it so hard for you to remember my name, Veronica? Is it because Danish people don't like Jews?"

Rob's father Mario, a silent Sicilian, refilled his wife's Mamajuana glass. He carved up big, cheesy pieces of lasagna and started passing them around to his three sons, who sat to his left.

Mom: "Martin. Give them some chicken."

He looked at the blackened bird, which sat blasted and reeking in front of him. He cut a small chunk out with his knife and peered at it.

Mom: "And salad!"

My brother took some salad and chicken. I passed my plate to Rob's dad, who loaded it up with lasagna, meatballs, beans and rice, and precariously topped the pile off with two hunks of bread. I dug in. My mother, to my right, stared at me with unconcealed contempt, her face barely an inch from my cheek. I ignored her. She was a champion close-starer.

I plowed through my plate of food, listening to my family crunch their way through charred chicken skin and raw onions. Rob's youngest brother sat in front of a nearly untouched plate of food. His mother stared blearily at him, her face bright red from Mamajuana.

Victoria: "Antony? What's a matta? You're Antony, right?"

Anthony: "I didn't really like the sausage. Or the meatballs. The lasagna isn't as good as usual either. It tastes like ginger."

My mother smirked proudly.

Me: "Oh my God, Ma. You didn't!"

Mom: "Have some chicken! And salad!"

Anthony's eyes widened in horror. My mouth was full, but my plate was empty. I handed it to him and motioned for him to pass me his. I put it in front of me and started eating. Anthony chuckled.

Me: "Laugh all you want, boy. You can go home with them. You'll be back in a day and a half, reeking of red onions and despair, soaked in your own urine. You'll hack off your own pinky finger for a piece of your mother's substandard lasagna." I forked half a meatball into my mouth.

My mother smacked the back of my head.

Mom: "SSSStace. How can you eat that crap?"

Victoria: *"Puta!"*

Mom: "I'm sure it's fine, Wilma. If you like that kind of thing."

Layne the Favorite stared wistfully at my food. I took his plate and upended it. Ashy chicken and onion salad slid onto the tablecloth. I put it back down flat, jabbed a meatball and dunked it in front of him.

Mom: "Layner! Don't you dare!"

Layne the Favorite dropped his fork glumly. I snatched the meatball back and took a huge bite.

16

MAROONED AT TURKEY LAKE

MY MOTHER HAD no use for college, and she had a very good reason:

Mom: "Your *brother* doesn't need college."

Me: "Because he's already perfect in every way?"

Mom: "Exactly!" She patted Layne the Favorite's cheek. He beamed.

Me: "Am I already perfect?"

My mother pursed her lips and looked over her half-glasses at me.

Mom: "I wouldn't say that. You know, SSSSStace, you're a lot like your father."

Me: "I've heard. You don't think college will beat that out of me?"

Mom: "Not likely, Buster. Do they still have jobs in coal mines or slaughterhouses you could get? Are the Goyim still building pyramids by hand? Our people are very good at that."

I went to college anyway, but because of the lack of support at home, I left for Florida State with only $20 in my pocket, driving a 1978 Volare. In December of 1988, my friend Rob and I went home for winter break. We loaded a sackful of homemade Big Macs into the car, and readied ourselves for eight hours of driving followed by three weeks of hard earned vacation. Smooth sailing.

Four hours later, we were broke and hungry, sitting in a dead car, waiting for Layne the Favorite to come save us.

We were doomed.

***

Rob was mad at me long before the car died and we ran out of food. We had signed up to be roommates in a dorm at FSU, but when we went to look at our room with his parents the July after graduation, there were issues.

I had lived in a motor home for five years, and since then, I've measured every space in terms of how many Winnebagos it could hold.

I use these measurements for comparison:

1. My current living room = 1 Winnebago
2. My current basement = 3 Winnebagos
3. The Rotunda of the US Capitol = 34 Winnebagos
4. Grand Central Station = 147 Winnebagos
5. Dorm room at Florida State = Less than 1 Winnebago

I stared at the tiny room, my eyes wide, sweat beading up on my forehead.

Rob's Mom: "Roberto. Your white Jewish friend! He looks even whiter! Even Jewisher! Get im a matzo ball or someting!"

Rob: "What's wrong with you?"

Me (in a panicked whisper): "Not one. Not even one!"

The room was smaller than my old recreational vehicle. I freaked and fled into the hallway. (Five Winnebagos, that hallway. I could have lived *there*, if it hadn't smelled like my mother's broiled fish and artichoke hearts. Hard to describe. Imagine the dessicated uvula of a man dying of thirst in the Sahara. That's what it smelled like).

Rob was, and still is an eternal optimist. Although we had to take turns entering and exiting and there was no air conditioning, he looked around the small space, ignoring the large pool of sweat forming around his feet, and said brightly, "This will be GREAT!"

The drive from Tallahassee back to Hollywood, where we lived, took nearly nine hours. His parents spent the entire time trying to talk him out of living in the dorm.

I stayed silent. I was firmly on his parents' side of the issue:

1. They were already paying for his brother's apartment in the same town. The additional expense of a dorm didn't make sense.
2. They were much happier at the thought of him living with his responsible older brother than with me. (Wait. What?)
3. The room was like the solitary confinement box from every prison movie I'd ever seen.

My mother was actually happy about the lack of air conditioning:

Mom: "SSSSSStace. You don't need air conditioning. Do you know what air conditioning does to you?"

Me: "Prevents heat stroke, dehydration, and death?"

Mom: "Particles!"

Me: "What?"

Mom: "Particles! SSSSStace. You want to go to college and you don't know particles? Air conditioning sssssshoots particles into the air —"

Me: "Cold particles, Ma. On hot days."

Mom: "And then you breathe that crap in and it gets into your cells. Your hair will fall out. You'll get the runs!"

I ended up in a studio apartment with my friend Mark. Rob went begrudgingly to fulfill his filial duty. I was sucked in by the fact that the rent included free utilities and an air conditioner unit that we ran year round. There were times when the apartment was sixty degrees, flooded with cell-killing, diarrhea-causing particles.

Although none of us had ever experienced it, Rob became an expert on dorm living. I met up with him at our 8am Biology class, out of breath from my mile long walk to campus.

He smacked me in the back of the head.

Rob: "Enjoy the walk, you bastard?"

Me (wishing I had an inhaler): "It's healthful."

Rob: "Wouldn't have that problem in a dorm."

***

HE WOULD STOP by my frigid apartment, silent and brooding, stalking around, poking his head into the kitchen, the closet, the tiny bathroom. He looked in the cupboards over the stove.

Rob: "Grocery shopping sucks, huh?"

Mark: "It's not so —"

Me: "That was a rhetorical question. Don't encourage him."

Rob: "Wouldn't have that problem in a dorm."

He looked at the mountain of dirty dishes in the sink, his arms folded.

Rob: "Want me to wash these for you?"

Mark: "That'd be great!"

Me: "Oh, Good Lord."

Rob: "Don't have to do dishes in a dorm..."

Me: "Did you stop by for a reason?"

This was a situation that required delicacy and tact. I was sure that Rob and I could get back on friendly terms if I extended a carefully crafted olive branch. So I offered him a ride home at Christmas, reminding him that he wouldn't have to drive with his brother.

All would be well again. As long as nothing went wrong.

✳✳✳

GROCERIES WERE EXPENSIVE and often perishable. There was no way we could leave food in the cupboards or the fridge while we were away for three weeks. We would have returned to a toxic mess. We had to eat it all, or throw it away.

Wouldn't have that problem in a dorm...

We stared at our inventory of hamburger patties, cheese, and buns. Mark, ever the planner, suggested that we make our own Big Macs. We had sixteen quarter pounders, thirty slices of yellow American (it was on sale), lettuce, and industrial sized jars of pickles, ketchup, and mayonnaise. According to the Big Mac theme song (which we studied like it was on our English final), all we needed were onions.

My mother, wherever she was at that moment, must have felt a rush of self-satisfied jubilation; there was always a big bag of onions in her house. She put them in everything. I hated them and refused to have them in the apartment.

Mark: "Too bad your mother —"

Me: "Just shut up and go get the onions."

***

WE ASSEMBLED EIGHT Big Macs, using a slice of Wonder Bread for the center bun. The empty bread bags were stuffed with the finished products and put away for the next day's journey. That night we feasted on omelets, celery stalks, grape juice, grilled chicken, yogurt, and cottage cheese. Then we cleaned the apartment until midnight.

***

I DROVE MY Volare in a sleepy haze to Rob's apartment the next morning, a bag of four homemade Big Macs on the seat next to me. Mark followed in his orange Impala. He had the other four.

Rob threw his bag in the back seat and walked to the driver's side door.

Me: "What?"

Rob: "Get out. If you drive, we won't get there until New Year's."

Me: "Am I the only one who took those videos they showed us in Driver's Ed seriously?"

Rob: "Move it."

I was about to remind him of the time he drove us to Orlando and fell asleep at the wheel, only waking up when the car plowed into the median strip on its way toward oncoming traffic, but decided not to; this drive home was a diplomatic mission. I slid over to the passenger seat. He got in, racked the seat back, and made himself comfortable. His elbow landed on the Big Mac bag. He stared at it.

Rob: "What are those?"

Me: "Big Macs. Homemade."

He got out of the car with the bag, walked over to Mark's car, and passed them through the driver's side window to him. He came back to the Volare and put the car in drive.

Rob: "You guys are weird."

I remained silent. Diplomatically silent.

***

By 11 AM, we had passed Gainesville and were approaching the entrance to the Florida Turnpike. I had just enough cash to pay for the tolls and the two tanks of gas we would need to get all the way back to Hollywood.

Rob: "We'll get some real food once we get on the Turnpike. Homemade Big Macs. Weirdos."

I pretended to be asleep, a time honored tradition in the diplomatic corps. Churchill was a master at it. That's how we won the big war. I was hoping for nothing less than restoring peace in our time. All we had to do was get home safely.

The Volare's engine whined like it was trying to launch us into orbit.

Rob: "What the fuck was that?"

I kept my eyes closed, wondering what Churchill would have done. Rob smacked me in the back of the head. The car drifted to a halt.

We had made it to the Service Plaza at Turkey Lake.

***

WHENEVER I'M ON the Florida Turnpike these days, I make a point of stopping at the Turkey Lake Service Plaza. I took my kids there once.

Caitlyn: "Dad. Why are we stopping? You've got the bladder of a kitten."

Erin: "A kitten with one kidney."

Today, the Service Plaza at Turkey Lake is a whitewashed palace: it has a Burger King, a Sbarro's, frigid air conditioning spewing particles into the unsuspecting cellular structure of hapless travelers, free wireless internet, and a men's room with eight clean, blindingly white urinals. The vending machines (both Coke and Pepsi) take credit cards as well as the currencies of three nations.

In 1988, it boasted of a Sunoco gas station, one broken Coke machine, and a dirty unisex bathroom where nothing flushed. Ever. It was run by Rusty the Mechanic, a sixty-something, sunburned, lanky fellow in grease-stained overalls and a cap that shielded his ice-blue eyes.

He glared at us over the hood of the Volare. Rob had sat behind the wheel while I pushed the car up the ramp to the Sunoco. Rusty the Mechanic met us outside. The temperature was nearing ninety. Christmas in Florida.

Rusty the Mechanic: "It doesn't look good, boys."

Rob: "What's wrong with it?"

Rusty the Mechanic: "Looks like the plasmicophic ferangiclink got mangled up in the left trigalamilling belt, which snapped like a slutty bride's garter. Then *that* got chewed up by the alloidal crantagulator, which caused the flipperintandicle to go all out of whack."

I'm sure that's what he said. All I understood was *slutty bride's garter*. I'm still no good with cars.

Rob: "Can you fix it?"

Rusty the Mechanic: "Pretty sure."

Rob: "How much will it cost?"

Rusty the Mechanic: "How much you got?"

Rob had three hundred dollars in cash that he had managed to save up from his part-time college job. He handed it over with all of my remaining money.

***

WE STOOD IN silence, grateful for the shade provided by the overhanging roof of the outbuilding where the one bathroom was. The stench from inside poured out like the pureed intestines of tortured heretics, or my mother's pea soup.

It was around two in the afternoon when Rusty the Mechanic slammed the hood closed and stepped back.

Rusty the Mechanic: "There you go, fellas. Have a good trip home."

We staggered to the car and got back in. Rob started it up and headed toward the Turnpike. The car died forever halfway down the on ramp. I got to push it backwards this time.

* * *

RUSTY THE MECHANIC had seen this sort of thing before.

Rusty the Mechanic: "One in a million, boys. The seal on the gadflagel must have cracked like a walnut. So your dipnothratic fluid just pours straight into the ulterior hugomisflick like a toilet flushing."

I'm sure that's what he said. I understood *cracked like a walnut*, but put no stock in his toilet flushing analogy - I'd seen the hellish inside of Rusty the Mechanic's ghastly restroom.

Me: "Can it be fixed?"

Rob: "No."

Rusty the Mechanic: "Well, son, you're gonna need a whole new lower hypergorangial, plus the alternate quixolactal is probably burned up like your momma's Thanksgiving turkey."

Me: "You have no idea. Where's your phone?"

***

WE DIDN'T HAVE any change for the pay phone, so I had to call Layne the Favorite collect. He was always home during the day: he and my mother had bought a bread delivery route as soon as I left for college. They had two cargo vans they drove around at four in the morning after packing up daily bread orders for restaurants in the dead of night.

Robotic Operator: "Will you accept the charges from...Stacey?"

Layne the Favorite: "No." Click. His mother had told him never to accept collect calls because it might have been our father calling from jail. Our father had never been to jail, but such fabrications were essential to divorce in the seventies.

Rob: "I'll call my dad. He'll be here in two and a half hours. Tops."

Which was true. Rob's dad was a man of few words and lots of action. All he needed to know was where we were.

Me: "No. It's my stupid car with its broken undercraffed glicksmid-ditch that got us into this mess."

Robotic Operator: "Will you accept the charges from... GODDAMMIT YOU BETTER PICK UP!"

Layne the Favorite: "Um...sure."

I explained the situation.

Layne the Favorite: "Tell the mechanic to check the left rollogoslog. Maybe the truncated protoskigger."

Me: "Just get in the damned van and come get us."

Layne the Favorite: "Okay. I'm on my way."

I hung up the phone and grinned at Rob. We were saved.

***

WE SAT IN the dead Volare, staring dully out the mosquito-stained windshield at the baked parking lot. We were hungry and dry as a desert. I had thought of drinking from the rusted, crusty bathroom faucet but lost my nerve. Despite the open windows and our dehydration, sweat poured off of us. It reminded me of the few minutes we had spent in the dorm. All semester could have been like this. I didn't share this thought with Rob.

Rob looked at his watch.

Rob: "It's almost six. He should be here by now. Unless he drives like you."

Me: "I'm sure he'll be here any minute. I should have told him to bring drinks." I didn't mention food - we had started this trip with Big Macs that he had given away.

Rob: "Call your mom and find out when he left."

I staggered to the payphone and leaned heavily against it.

Robotic Operator: "Will you accept the charges from...<u>I'm dying out here!</u>"

Layne the Favorite: "Sure!"

Me: "What are you still DOING there?"

Layne the Favorite: "I'm waiting for Uncle Julius to get here."

Uncle Julius was eighty years old. He had lived through the Great Depression and marrying into our family. He was a good man to have in a crisis, but all I needed was a ride.

Me: "Why are you waiting for him?"

Layne the Favorite: "I'm not going to drive by myself."

Me: "Just get in the car and move it!"

Layne the Favorite: "Okay. You really need to calm down."

I hung up.

At seven thirty, Rob looked at his watch.

Rob: "Call home again."

I didn't even argue.

Robotic Operator: "Will you accept the charges from...<u>you better not fucking be there!</u>"

Layne the Favorite: "Sure!"

Me: "Oh. My. GOD! Why are you still there?"

Layne the Favorite: "We had to have dinner. Mom made stuffed cabbage. Hang on. She wants to talk to you."

My mother's stuffed cabbage tasted like a condemned killer's frantic pleas for mercy. For a moment I was grateful to be slowly starving to death in the middle of Florida.

Me: "I swear to God, if you don't get in your fucking car RIGHT NOW —"

Mom: "SSSSStace. What are you doing?"

Me: "Dying. Slowly. With my friend Rob."

Mom: "Rick? Who's this Rick? I never heard of him."

Me: "Rob."

Mom: "That's what I said. When are you going to be here? I made stuffed cabbage."

Me: "Our car broke down."

Mom: "No it didn't."

I banged my forehead against the pay phone. I didn't feel a thing. I was dying for sure.

Me: "Didn't Layne tell you? He said he was going to come pick us up."

Mom: "Oh, that's right. That's what he was talking about. Sometimes I don't get what other people are saying, SSSSStace. It's the arsenic poisoning."

Me: "You know he's going to have to actually leave the house to come get me, right?"

Mom: "SSSSSStace. What is wrong with you? Of course he's leaving the house."

Me (in a dehydrated whisper): "When? For God's sake, when?"

Mom: "In a few minutes. We gotta do the dishes first."

Me: "You've got to be kidding me."

Mom: "SSStace. You know what happens if you leave dirty dishes out? They get bacteria. Bacteria breeds bugssss."

Me: "Bugs breed bugs, Ma."

Mom: "Sssso. All of a sudden you're a scientist?"

Me: "Just get him in the car. I'll do the dishes when I get home."

Mom: "I don't believe that. You never do the dishes."

Me: "Can you put him on the phone?"

Mom: "Sure. Have fun."

Me: "Layne. Get in the car right now and come get me and I'll give you a hundred bucks. If you don't, I swear to God I will kill you if it's the last thing I ever do."

Layne the Favorite: "All right already! What is *wrong* with you?"

I hung up. I sat on the trunk of the car.

Rob: "Still hasn't left, has he?"

I pretended to be asleep.

* * *

ROB WAS SNORING behind the wheel at nine o'clock when I went back to the pay phone:

Robotic Operator: "Will you accept charges from...<u>just kill me now</u>."

Layne the Favorite: "Sure!"

Me: "Just don't bother coming to get us. You'll need the extra time to pack everything you own and start running so I don't ever find you."

Layne the Favorite: "You're so ungrateful. We got the van all packed up and ready to go. Mom made you guys some sandwiches. Just relax, will you?"

He hung up.

***

It was nearly midnight when the white van pulled up behind the Volare. Layne the Favorite got out and went to the driver's side window. Rob glared at him.

Layne the Favorite: "Pop the hood, will you, Bob? I think it's just the yangercracktal. Two seconds to fix. I can't believe you guys sat here all day for one little grobbelflanger."

Rob got out of the car, grabbed his bag, and walked wordlessly to the back of the cargo van. He got in and leaned against the metal wall like he was part of a prisoner transfer. I followed him. We sat on the floor near the back doors. My mother and Uncle Julius were in the only available seats. My mother rummaged through her purse and handed us sandwiches wrapped in plastic. Even with that covering I could smell the raw red onions. Rob took his sandwich from her and with the same fluid movement tossed it out the open back door of the van. I sent mine after it. It was too dark for my mother to see. Rob pulled the door closed.

Layne the Favorite opened the back door of the van.

Layne the Favorite: "Well. If you want to leave the car here, we should at least take the tires and the radio and the —"

There was a plastic tray that they used to haul bread digging into my thigh. I picked it up and swung it as hard as I could at him. It smashed to pieces an inch from his head.

Layne the Favorite: "Hey!"

Me: "Just drive us home."

Layne the Favorite: "Someone's awfully touchy today."

I looked around for another bread tray. He hurriedly slammed the door shut.

* * *

WE MADE IT to Rob's house at two-thirty in the morning. Nearly three hours of sitting on the ribbed metal floor of the van had turned us into solid, cranky bruises. His dad heard the van coming and was waiting outside.

Rob: "Oh, good. My dad's awake. He's going to kill every last one of you."

Mom: "Ask him if he wants a sandwich!"

Rob got out of the van before it stopped completely. His father took his bag and wrapped his arm around him. I heard him telling Rob that he could have been at Turkey Lake twelve hours earlier.

The van door slammed. I had a very clear sense that diplomatic relations had broken down. Over the next twenty-five years though,

Rob and I remained the best of friends - he is godfather to my kids and I am godfather to his, though he won't let me drive them anywhere.

Maybe one day he and I and our kids can take a nostalgic trip back to the Turkey Lake Service Plaza for old time's sake. We can visit the site of the unkillable weeds that once grew in the spot where we had tossed my mother's sandwiches.

On the other hand, maybe it's better if we don't.

17

BLOOD FROM A STONE

I'VE TAKEN A number of sharp blows to the head throughout my career as a clumsy child:

1. Rammed into a gate when Layne the Favorite slammed into my bike at top speed.
2. Hit a Pontiac with my face after my bike's front tire hit the car's back bumper.
3. Knocked out my own front teeth with my knees after jumping off a roof to land on a serial killer's cast-off mattresses.
4. Struck the windshield of a Cadillac with my head after its decrepit driver ran a red light outside the trailer park I lived in.

So it was easy to think that I would suffer some cumulative effect of all this neurological damage and start hallucinating. Especially in the summer of 1989 when I thought my mother said:

"SSSSSStace. I'm giving you a car."

***

I COULDN'T HAVE heard her right. My mother has been known to give plenty of vehicles away, but never to me. At the time she made this announcement, I was eighteen, carless, and done with my first year of college at Florida State University. The only car I ever had, my beloved Volare, had died forever at the Florida Turnpike Service Plaza at Turkey Lake. My roommate's car died on the way back to FSU that winter, so we pooled our resources to buy a moped, which was used to cart our groceries. It was a squeaky, rattling death trap.

Layne the Favorite, on the other hand, had five vehicles bestowed upon him before I was even old enough to drive:

1. A red Dodge Dart, which was destroyed when he was hit by an old man going the wrong way around Young's Circle in Hollywood, Florida. The day nearly ended in Layne's arrest when he told the police officer on the scene that he was "going to go over there and punch the old fart's lights out."

2. A wood paneled Ford, which was destroyed forever when he slammed it into reverse at fifty miles an hour on Taft Street, just to see what would happen. As it turns out, something called "a transmission" dropped into the middle of the road and the car stopped for good.

3. A scooter, which was no good to drive in the rain. He rolled it into a canal and watched triumphantly as it sank. He later told my mother that it was just as well. He needed to be dry.

4. My Uncle Julius's Chevy Caprice, lovingly maintained, an iron horse of a car, handed over with all of Julius's other worldly possessions when he came to live with us. We later found out that cars do not run without "oil."

5. A Ford Econoline van, which my mother and brother used on their bread delivery route. This was the vehicle used to extract me from the Turkey Lake Service Plaza after the Volare met its end. My mother reminded Layne as often as

she could that this van was the basis of their financial future, and should be well cared for. His response: "It's a piece of shit."

I was lost in this envious reverie (or suffering latent brain trauma from my skull-cracking childhood). My mother had no patience for woolgathering or neurological damage.

Mom: "SSSStace. Why don't you answer me? You never listen. What is *wrong* with you?"

Me: "I guess Layne would like another car, sure."

Mom: "Not him. You."

Me: "Did I get hit in the head recently? Is this what a stroke feels like?"

Mom: "Getting hit in the head is no big deal, Buster."

While I was away at college, Layne the Favorite had gotten hit alongside the bridge of his nose with a baseball at one of the games he played with other guys from the bread company. My mother had him at a neurologist's office before nightfall.

Me: "Maybe I should go see Layne's neurologist."

Mom: "There's nothing wrong with you."

Me: "Then why do you keep asking what's wrong with me?"

Mom: "Because there's definitely something wrong with you. I just don't know what it is."

TRAILER TRASH, WITH A GIRL'S NAME

Me: "Time to get a professional on the case, don't you think?"

Mom: "College isn't working for you, Buster. Do you want the Saab or not?"

The Saab was white, four years old, with heated seats that no one in our part of Florida ever needed. The ignition was between the seats, and when you started it up, the engine purred and the interior lights lit up like the night sky over Sweden. It was sleek and modern, and I always thought that when I grew up and got a job, I would get a car just like it.

Me: "Yes. I will absolutely take the car."

Layne the Favorite glared at me from the couch.

Layne the Favorite: "I don't know why *he* gets to take it."

Mom: "Hush, Layner. You know why."

***

I WAS ALLOWED to take the Saab with me to college for none of these reasons:

1. I had graduated seventh in my senior class, which was "no reason to give you a medal or anything, smart guy. You wouldn't have even made it through high school if your brother didn't drive you back and forth every day."

2. I had gotten an honest-to-God medal when I was in my high school's ROTC program. The Superior Cadet medal is recognized by the Department of the Army as an actual military decoration, unlike the other ones we received, none of which

would have happened if "your brother didn't drive you to all these *facochta* ROTC events, Buster."

3. I was the first person in my family to go to college, "and you'd still be stuck there if your brother hadn't driven up there in the middle of the night to get you when your car broke down."

In fact, according to my mother's version of events, I was nothing without a ride. You would think a car would be a brilliant solution to all my shortcomings.

The real answer as to why I was getting the car lay in the phone call that came the next morning. I was the only one in the house; my mother and Layne the Favorite were delivering bread in the van that we all fervently hoped would survive my brother's regime.

Weary Collections Agent: "This is Saab Motor Credit. Can I speak with Carol, please?"

Me: "She's not home."

Weary Collections Agent: "Is this her husband?"

Me: "No. He's dealing drugs in California. I'm her son."

Weary Collections Agent: "The one in college, or the one she likes?"

Me (warily): "The one in college."

Weary Collections Agent: "Oh thank God. Can you pass a message along to your mother, please?"

Me: "You seem to know a lot about us for a car company."

Weary Collections Agent: "We're the financing arm of Saab. We're handling the note on your mother's 1984 Saab. I've had a lot of conversations with Carol." He sounded like he was about to cry. Or kill himself.

Me: "Me too."

Weary Collections Agent: "We are willing to take her remaining payments and re-amortize the note over five years. It'll lower her payments to ninety-six dollars a month."

Me: "No way. That's a great deal."

Weary Collections Agent: "We don't want the car back. Can you encourage her to accept the terms we're offering?"

Me: "If you've had so many conversations with her, why haven't you been able to get her to agree?"

Weary Collections Agent: "If you've had so many conversations with her, I'm sure *you* know why."

Me: "Ah, yes. Blood from a stone."

Weary Collections Agent (holding back tears): "Blood from a stone."

* * *

YOU COULD GET manna from heaven. You could get oil to light the menorah. Moses, our people's greatest prophet, managed to get water from a rock. But you could never get blood from a stone. It was a lesson I learned early:

1. The Hebrew school where I went for elementary school was demanding a tuition payment, or they were going to throw me out. Dreading public school, I asked why my mother couldn't pay the tuition. Her answer should've been that she was recently

divorced and my father was a deadbeat and she was starting her own business, but it wasn't.

2. Our water got shut off for non-payment. She owed thirty dollars. She sent us out into the night with buckets we filled at our neighbors' unguarded garden hoses. The notices from the water company went in the trash unopened.

3. We were about to get evicted from our trailer park in San Diego. They had failed to record the payment she had made for the prior month. They left letters taped to the door of our RV, which got ripped up. We finally pulled up stakes one morning before dawn and left for Lake Tahoe.

4. She started a beauty salon with a gin-swilling, till-stealing, frizzy-haired monster. Once her partner skipped out on her, my mother refused to open the shop. The company that sold her all of her equipment and the landlord of her new location joined forces and sued her. They offered to settle for half of what she owed them. She ignored them and went bankrupt.

5. One day in 1989 she decided not to pay for her Saab any more, ten months before it was completely paid off.

Me: "Mom. I got a call from the Saab people today."

Mom: "SSSSSStace. Did you tell them they can't get blood from a stone?"

Me: "I think they already knew. It was your old pal Gary. He said they could wrap your remaining payments into a five year note."

Mom: "I hope you told Glenn that there's no way. Blood from a stone!"

Me: "Gary."

Mom: "That's what I said!"

Me: "They really don't want the car back."

Mom (teeth gritted): "SSSSSStace. They're not getting the god-damned car."

Me: "Then just pay them. They're asking for less money than Layne's bowling league membership costs."

Mom: "SSSStace. Your brother is an excellent bowler. His team needs him. You know where they'd be without him?"

Me: "First place?"

Mom: "Last place! So I'm paying whatever it costs. It's good for him. You take the *facochten* car to college and those *momsers* won't get their hands on it."

***

EVER THE OPTIMIST, I looked on the bright side. I got the car of my dreams to drive around in all summer, and then I was taking it back to college with me. No more death trap moped. Shortly after this bequest, I got a financial aid check for the fall term - almost four thousand dollars. It was nearly enough to pay off the Saab and keep it for myself without fear of repossession. If my new friend Gary from Saab hadn't already killed himself and called back, I would accept his offer on my mother's behalf, find out where to mail the check, and keep the car. She would never have to know. All of her stones would remain unbloodied.

The phone rang. I leapt for it.

Me: "Gary?"

Weary Mortgage Collector: "Um...no, sir. This is Sun Trust Mortgage. Is Carol home?"

Me: "No. I'm her son."

Weary Mortgage Collector: "How's the bread business?"

Me: "The other one."

Weary Mortgage Collector: "You know, I never went to college and I turned out just fine."

Me: "Can I help you with something?"

Weary Mortgage Collector: "I'm hoping you can pass along our latest settlement offer to your mother. She's four months past due with her mortgage payment and she has resisted every attempt we've made to work this out —"

Me: "Blood from a stone."

Weary Mortgage Collector: "Yeah. Is that some kind of Bible thing? Like manna from heaven?"

Me: "No. You can actually get manna from heaven. Also, apparently, water from rocks."

Weary Mortgage Collector: "Fascinating. Anyway, we will stop all foreclosure activity and start a full refinance of the property if she will send us $4000 by close of business Friday."

I looked at my financial aid check.

Me: "What address should I send it to?"

***

ME: "SSSSSSSo. MOM. The mortgage?"

Mom: "I told them! Blood from a stone!"

Me: "I paid it already. They're going to call about a refinancing. You better just do what they want."

Mom: "No way! Can you get blood from a stone, SSSStace? Can you?"

Me (wearily): "They did today."

I left the house and headed for the car. The gently glowing interior of the Saab would be heavenly. In another week I would be driving it back to college. I walked the two blocks to the parking space in another part of the subdivision we lived in where I had been hiding the Saab from the repossession squad.

It was gone.

18

RIGHT SHIKSA, WRONG SON

I HAD STALLED as long as I could but time had run out. I had no choice. It was enough already.

Mom: "SSSSSStace. Enough already. You've been living with this girl for months. You need to bring Carla over to meet your mother."

Me: "Kim."

Mom: "That's what I said. Bring her Friday night. I'll make dinner."

Me: "Couldn't we have dinner out somewhere?" I was totally broke, but I would have sold a kidney to pay for a dinner she didn't cook.

Mom: "No way, Buster. I can cook better than any *facochta* restaurant. We'll eat here. I'll make lasagna."

Me: "Lasagna? With meat?"

Mom: "Of course with meat. How can you make a lasagna without meat? What is *wrong* with you?"

Me: "Ma! Wait! What kind of meat?"

But she had hung up.

***

I STARED INTENTLY at Kim as she got ready for dinner at Mom's. I lowered my glasses and peered over them the way my mother did when she looked at me. Like Superman's X-ray vision, maybe this was the way to see past the outer layers and ferret out other people's flaws and shortcomings.

I must have been doing it wrong. She was a just a fast-moving blur.

Kim: "Why are you looking at me?"

I pursed my lips and tried my mother's classic look of disdain. Still nothing.

Kim: "You can wipe *that* fucking look off your face, too."

Me (sadly): "Get used to it."

Kim: "So what exactly are you trying to accomplish?"

Me: "I'm trying to figure out what's wrong with you."

Kim (an edge to her voice): "Absolutely nothing."

Me: "Impossible! There's a whole list of things. Come on. I need you to dig in here. She doesn't like blondes. Do we have enough time to color your hair?"

She shook her head.

Me: "You're still Catholic, right? She'll hate that."

Kim: "I don't go to church."

Me: "Oh, please. You think that will matter to her? What about the smoking?"

She was outside, standing by the open apartment door, a Marlboro between her lips, her face a misty blur behind a blue haze.

Kim: "I'm not going to quit, if that's what you're asking."

Me: "And your grandfather? Still German?"

Kim: "*Jawol.*"

Me (channeling my mother): "SSSSo. Your grandfather. The Nazi. You know he killed our people, right?"

Kim: "He served in the Navy during the war. On the American side."

Me (shaking my head): "We're just so screwed."

* * *

THERE WAS A moment while standing in front of the door to my mother's house when I wondered if I was supposed to ring the bell. Even though I had lived there through most of high school and part of college, I was coming back today as a dinner guest, with a woman. Grownups living in sin should ring the bell. Right?

Kim opened the door and walked straight in. Brazen *shiksa* hussy. My mom was going to hate that. I followed her inside, sure that from this moment forward the women were in charge.

TRAILER TRASH, WITH A GIRL'S NAME

***

As a child, I developed a habit of sniffing the air whenever I walked into my mother's house. I stayed close to the door, ready to flee if any of her standard cooking aromas attacked my nose:

1. Despair with crystallized ginger
2. Chicken
3. Hopelessness covered in paprika
4. Egg salad (no yolks, just the whites, with soy mayo)
5. Dill-encrusted misery
6. Red onions

On this night, her house smelled like an Italian bistro: tomato sauce, garlic, baking bread. I froze, inhaling and exhaling quickly, like a mentally-challenged squirrel.

Me: "No onions? Something's not right here. I don't smell any grief. Or even mild sadness." I debated turning around and running until my legs gave out.

Marvin, King of the Jews glared at me as I stood rooted to the spot, paralyzed by indecision. I was going to get a talking to.

***

My mother had been dating Marvin, King of the Jews for about six months. She had been technically single since Ted the Drug Dealer left for California midway through my second year of college, but I couldn't take of any of her subsequent suitors seriously. They were all men in their late eighties. My mother wasn't even fifty.

I met some of them when I was home from college:

Mom: "SSSSSStace. Come meet Hyman. You'll like him."

She said the same thing about her cooking, so I was skeptical.

Hyman the Octogenarian: "Nice to meet you, Stuart."

Me: "You too. Don't get up."

Hyman the Octogenarian (chuckling): "Oh, Steven, don't be silly. I can't get up."

Me: "Mom. Seriously?"

Mom: "SSSSStace. Hyman's a very interesting man."

Me: "Because he was drinking buddies with Warren G. Harding? How about that Teapot Dome thing, Hyman? A real bitch, am I right?"

Hyman the Octogenarian (shaking his head): "Ah, yes. Teapot Dome. Bad times. Bad times. Now, Herbert Hoover, he was a real President, Samuel. I wish we had a guy like him in the White House now."

Me: "And that we still use the telegraph."

Hyman the Octogenarian: "Simple is best. I don't bother with all this complicated technology. It's too much."

Me: "Push button phones, color TV, indoor plumbing, that sort of thing?"

Hyman the Octogenarian: "Exactly right, Sandy. Exactly. You know, you seem like a nice boy. I don't know why she dislikes you so much."

Me: "Give it time, Hyman. Give it time. I mean, however much time you have left."

There was also Sol the Pharmacist. He was seventy-six, and all he ever talked about were his meds. I came downstairs to find my mother at the kitchen table, counting pills of all sizes and hues into those segmented containers marked with the days of the week. One set was a full week of pills. My mother had nine.

Sol the Pharmacist sat across from her, arms folded. His skin was so pale it was nearly translucent. I expected to be able to see his writhing insides.

Mom: "Sol. You should have flaxseed oil."

Sol the Pharmacist pondered, then nodded. My mother started dropping flaxseed oil pellets into each of the daily squares. It sounded like she had hit the jackpot on a slot machine.

Me: "What's flaxseed oil good for?"

Mom: "SSSSSStace. It's loaded with antioxidants. It fights breast cancer. There was a study."

Me: "Worried much about breast cancer, Sol?"

Sol the Pharmacist (shrugging): "You never know. Carol. Don't forget the Garcina Cambogia Extract."

Me: "You're making that up."

Sol the Pharmacist: "It's good for the metabolism."

Me: "What for? You going on safari with Teddy Roosevelt?"

My mother continued putting multi-colored pills into Sol the Pharmacist's little boxes. His urine must have been the color of a leprechaun's rainbow.

Me: "Why bother with the pills? When it's your time to go, it's your time to go."

Sol the Pharmacist got even paler. My mother stared at me, speechless.

They broke up that same day. It took a panel truck to carry Sol's pills back to his condo.

***

BEHOLD: NOW COMETH unto the land Marvin, King of the Jews, sixty-two years old, tall, slender, slightly hunched over, gray haired, with large eyes magnified behind thick glasses. He had owned a TV repair shop in Miami Beach and was quite successful until his customers wanted him to work on the newfangled color sets. Then he was out.

He was very active in his temple, and knew everything there was to know about Judaism. I had been dragged to Passover dinner at my mother's house the year before. Marvin, King of the Jews was officiating.

Marvin, King of the Jews: "You know why we eat matzah on Passover?"

Me: "Yes. Because when the Israelites fled slavery in Egypt, they —"

Marvin, King of the Jews: "The crunchiness reminds us of the sand we used to make bricks for our Egyptian overseers."

Me: "Um...it was because there was no time to let the bread rise before the Jews had to leave in the middle of the night to escape the Pharaoh's troops."

My mother and Marvin, King of the Jews stared at me.

Mom: "The crunchiness, SSSSSStace. The crunchiness!"

Me: "Did we *eat* the fucking sand?"

Marvin, King of the Jews: "You don't know anything about Jewish history, young man. You should come to Temple. Your brother goes. He's such a good boy."

Layne the Favorite nodded smugly, crunching his way through some matzah.

I grabbed the bottle of Manischevitz wine, filled my glass, and drained it.

Me: "Marvin. You know why we drink wine at Passover?"

Marvin, King of the Jews (disdainfully): "Of course. It reminds us of when God turned the Red Sea to blood, and then parted it so the Israelites could escape the Egyptian chariots."

I gulped another glass of wine. I felt overcome with grapey serenity.

Me (blissfully): "That's not why."

Marvin, King of the Jews: "I just don't know what's wrong with you."

Me: "Welcome to the family. Can someone pass me whatever it is that reminds us of the bitter tears we shed while held captive by our oppressors?"

***

KIM WENT TO the kitchen and introduced herself to my mother, who stepped back and stared at her over the top of her glasses, her lips pursed. I sprinted over and stood next to her, staring at my girlfriend.

My mother and I remained side by side for a few seconds, like bird-watchers trying to decide if we had discovered an unknown species.

Me (whispering): "What do you see?"

My mother turned and looked at me.

Mom: "What are you talking about? Kathy seems very nice."

Me: "Kim."

Mom: "That's what I said. Katie, you do like lasagna, don't you?"

Kim: "Sure. I love it."

Me: "What's in the lasagna, Ma?"

Mom: "Never you mind, Buster."

Me: "We could go out for dinner. I'll pay! A second kidney's really just redundant self indulgence anyway."

Kim and my mother stared at me, and asked the same question at the same time:

"What is *wrong* with you?"

Marvin, King of the Jews: "There's plenty wrong with him. Come here, young man. I need to talk to you."

Oh, boy.

***

MARVIN, KING OF the Jews was a close talker. He stood barely six inches away and leaned down, staring at me with his magnified eyes.

Marvin, King of the Jews: "This really hurts me, you know."

Me: "Maybe you should stand up straighter. Hunching over like that must be killing your back."

Marvin, King of the Jews: "You've been dating this girl, the *shiksa* with the big boobs, for how long?"

Me: "A few months."

Marvin, King of the Jews: "And this is the first time you bring her to meet me? And your mother?"

Me: "Well, we've been pretty busy —"

Marvin, King of the Jews: "You know, in the Bible, when any of the prophets or kings wanted to get married, they brought the women to meet their parents."

Me: "We're not getting married."

Marvin, King of the Jews (shaking his head sadly): "Yes. The living in sin. It's very disappointing. Do you know how much that hurts me? And your mother?"

Me: "*You're* living in sin."

Mom: "Dinner's ready."

That was the first time in recorded history when I was happy to hear those words.

***

THERE WAS A huge salad bowl in the middle of the table. I poked at it with my fork. Everyone was horrified. Kim kicked me under the table.

Mom: "SSSSStace. What are you doing?"

Me: "There are no onions in here."

Mom: "I can cut some up if you want them."

Me: "Never mind."

After the salad, she dished up plates of lasagna. I peered at it. I wished I had a lab I could send it to for analysis, but there just wasn't enough time, and it was Friday night. All the decent labs were probably closed.

Me: "There's cheese on this. It looks like real cheese."

Mom: "Of course there's cheese on it. How do you make a lasagna without cheese?"

Me: "I mean it's not soy cheese, or cheese made from recycled cardboard."

Mom: "That wouldn't be good on a lasagna."

Me: "You used it in the lasagna we had last year."

Mom: "No I didn't."

She did. It had tasted like the body odor of Attilla the Hun's cavalry. They made their clothes out of sewn-together mouse skins,

never changed them, never bathed (except in the blood of their ene-
mies), and slept on horseback.

Mom: "Christine. Would you like another piece?"

Kim: "I'd love one."

Me (whispering): "Don't do it. You haven't had time to build up an
immunity."

My mother passed her plate, and Kim took it. Then the interview
started.

✻✻✻

Mom: "SSSSSSo. Constance. You go to college?"

Kim nodded.

Mom: "And you work? Two jobs, right? You're a dispatcher at a bus
company and you're an EMT at night?"

That was more than my mother knew about me.

Mom: "You seem very ambitiousssssss. That's good." She looked
at me. "You know, SSSStace. I think she'd be a great match for your
brother."

Marvin, King of the Jews: "Absolutely. He needs someone who has
ambition. A good job. A direction in life. An education."

Me: "What would Mom do with all that free time?"

Mom: "Candace would be perfect for him."

Me: "Don't you think she'd be perfect for *me*?"

Marvin, King of the Jews: "Not really. She'd definitely be better off with Layne."

Me: "Are you kidding me? Look at her! She's blonde! And who really needs boobs that big? You know she's Catholic, right? And a smoker! Her grandfather was a Nazi, for God's sake! A Nazi!"

Kim was kicking me so hard under the table that my leg had gone numb.

Mom: "SSSSSStace. What are you talking about? Her grandfather was in the Navy. The *American* Navy. And she doesn't go to church anyway. Honestly, I'm surprised you know so little about your own girlfriend. It's disgussssssting. Your brother would pay more attention to her. He *listens*. Not like you."

Marvin, King of the Jews: "You're just like your father."

Kim: "That son of a bitch? I've heard a lot about that guy."

Me: "Do we have any Manischevitz?"

✳✳✳

I LIMPED TO the door. My mother hugged Kim.

Mom: "It was very nice to meet you, Kim."

Me: "Her name's Kim, Mom."

Kim: "That's what she said."

Me: "Right. Must be the Manischevitz. Or the leg trauma."

Mom: "What are you talking about?"

Marvin, King of the Jews: "You should definitely come back and meet his brother. He's such a good boy."

Me: "Can we go now?"

* * *

WE DROVE HOME in silence for a while.

Kim: "They weren't that bad."

I didn't say anything. I was concentrating on driving.

Kim: "And the lasagna was pretty good. I'm starting to wonder if all those stories you told me about her lousy cooking weren't true. You do tend to exaggerate, you know."

Me (bitterly): "I'll bet my dad was prone to hyperbole too."

Kim: "Pull over!"

Me: "We're on the highway. I can't get over."

She reached down to the floor and rooted around. She finally came up with one of those narrow plastic bags newspapers come in. She held it over her mouth and vomited explosively. The bag filled up.

I cut across three lanes of traffic to the shoulder. She opened the door and flopped out of the car, throwing up in the grass along the side of the road. I got out of the car, walked around to her side, carefully extracted the full bag of puke, and pitched it far away. I tried to help her, but she waved me away, retching and weeping.

After a few minutes, she managed to get back in the car, her cheeks wet and her breath foul. I opened the windows and headed for home.

Kim and I got divorced after ten years of marriage. I have a sneaky feeling that when my mother heard the news, she put a lasagna in the oven and told my brother to put on his best *shmatah*.

Mom: "Layner. We're having a guest for dinner. You'll like her."

19

FAT CHANCE

I come from a long line of short, stubby people who can't cook. You would think this would make us skinny, but no such luck. After exhaustive research, I found the syndrome that explains it.

I am a refugee eater.

***

In my religion, boys become men at thirteen. Not by getting drunk, cavorting with whores, or joining some sort of military force. Instead, we have to sit through months of instruction with a rabbi (who always smells of gefilte fish and onions) and then perform a dog and pony show (two non-kosher animals, that's for sure) on a bright Friday night in front of the whole congregation.

At least there are gifts. Jews are big fans of milestone events such as circumcisions, bar mitzvahs, and weddings. The gifts come pouring in, but only in response to pain, embarrassment, and misery. For Hanukkah, the only actual gift giving holiday we have, I get lottery tickets and those gold coins that turn out to be chocolate.

Which makes me fat.

Right around the time I turned thirteen, I noticed that I was not nearly as tall as I needed to be for my girth.

Me: "Mom. Is there any chance I might grow ten or twelve inches taller by my bar mitzvah?"

Mom: "SSSSSStace. What are you talking about? You'll never be six feet tall. You were a preemie. A preemie! You weighed two pounds when you were born. I thought you were a goner."

Me: "I was a Marlboro baby."

Mom: "Marlboro?"

Me: "Isn't that your cigarette of choice?"

Mom: "Smoking has nothing to do with preemies! I was a preemie. My sssssssister was a preemie."

Me: "But your mother didn't smoke, right?"

Mom: "Pack a day! Sometimes two."

Me: "And that has nothing to do with low birth weight?"

Mom (dangerously): "That's what your father kept asking."

Me: "Ah. Anyway. No chance of a height improvement?"

Mom: "No way, buster. Your brother, he'll be the tall one. And he'll have a nice head of hair."

Me: "Of course he will. So I guess I need to go on a diet."

Mom: "You should. You're getting zaftig. I'll have to start buying your clothes at Omar the Tentmaker."

***

I DIDN'T GET fat at home; I got fat at other people's houses. Like the time in elementary school when I was paired up with Stanislav the Cossack, a new student from the Ukraine who barely spoke any English. We had to work on a school project, so I went to his house. When I got there, his mother had prepared a plate of sandwiches and they offered me one.

I studied the sandwich carefully. The bread was white and square, with a golden crust around the edge. There was some kind of lunch meat in the middle. There were no red onions. I took a tentative bite. It was glorious.

Me: "What kind of sandwich is this?"

Stanislav the Cossack: "Baloney."

Me: "Oooh! A Ukrainian delicacy! And what kind of bread is that?"

He looked at his mother.

Mama Cossack: "Vonder Bread."

Me: "Wonder Bread. Good name for it. Is it some kind of special Ukrainian flour? How did they get it to be white? Are you allowed to make sandwiches without red onions in your country?"

They stared at me. I took advantage of their silence to eat the remaining sandwiches. I don't know how we fared on our school project, but I was never invited back.

***

As I GOT older, the problem (and my waistline) grew. During the seventies, a McDonald's hamburger was about thirty cents, so three of them could be had for less than a dollar. Money in those days was literally lying around: Ted the Drug Dealer had one of those coin belts where you pushed a plunger to make change. He wore it all the time, as if he was some kind of soldier with a cartridge belt, or maybe Batman. If I woke him up suddenly while he was napping, he would convulse and twitch. His gyrations would push the plunger, and coins would tumble to the floor. The bigger the shock, the more money I could get. I became an expert in the art of waking up Ted the Drug Dealer.

Layne the Favorite caught me at it one day.

Me: "Ted. The marijuana's on fire!"

Ted the Drug Dealer: "Wha? On fire? What?"

Cha-ching! Three dimes hit the floor. One McDonald's hamburger. Ted the Drug Dealer rolled over and snored.

Layne the Favorite: "What are you doing?"

Me: "Collecting the nap tax."

Layne the Favorite: "What for?"

Me: "To get money."

TRAILER TRASH, WITH A GIRL'S NAME

Layne the Favorite: "Mom gives me all the money I need. She's great, isn't she?"

Me: "You betcha. And where do you hide all that money?"

Layne the Favorite (proudly): "In my - hey!"

Me: "So close..."

Layne the Favorite: "You're just like your father."

Me: "That's what I hear. Ted! Mom's making liver for dinner!"

Ted the Drug Dealer fell off the couch onto the floor, looked around wildly, and sprinted for his cab. A lone nickel gleamed on the carpet.

Me (ruefully): "Must have been too big a scare." I headed to McDonald's.

***

I REALIZED MY weight had become a problem during one of my bar mitzvah boot camp sessions with Rabbi Goldshmear.

Me: "Forty days and forty nights seems like a long time."

Rabbi Goldshmear: "Especially in the desert. Although you could probably use some quality time out in the Sinai with just bread and water."

Me: "What do you mean?"

Rabbi Goldshmear: "You're getting a little zaftig. Has your mother gotten your bar mitzvah suit yet?"

Me: "Not yet. She's having it made by Omar the Tentmaker."

Rabbi Goldshmear laughed so hard that his face turned red and the air smelled like Bring Your Onions to Work Day at the gefilte fish plant.

Me: "Can't I just become a man the way the goyim do? Get drunk? Cavort with whores? Steal a car?"

Rabbi Goldshmear gasped a final oniony blast and stared at me uncomprehendingly. Then he got it.

Rabbi Goldshmear: "Ah, yes. Your father. He is a goy, is he not? Your mother says you want to be like him. It breaks her heart."

***

THAT WAS THE last straw. That very day I started jogging, which made me late for dinner.

Mom: "SSSSStace. Where were you? We ate an hour ago. Your kasha and bowties are probably ruined."

My mother's kasha and bowties tasted like the wretched tears of a first-day prison inmate after lights out.

Me: "I'm pretty sure they are. My fault. I'll just go to bed without any dinner."

Mom: "No way, Buster! I'll just zap them and they'll be fine!"

I had been living with the best diet plan ever made. As long as I only ate my mother's cooking (or avoided it, which was what I did most of the time), I'd drop all the weight I needed. Dinner at Mom's was the best appetite suppressant ever invented. Omar the Tentmaker was going out of business.

In the first week alone I lost nine pounds.

✳ ✳ ✳

My mother glared at me across the dinner table.

Mom: "SSSSSSSo. How's the fish?"

My mother's broiled monkfish with spinach smelled like a dumpster after a hard summer rain and tasted like the fetid breath of a street bum.

Me: "Great! Why?"

Mom: "You're up to something. Aren't you, smart guy?"

Me (with dewy-eyed innocence): "I have no idea what you're talking about."

Layne the Favorite: "I agree, Mother. He's up to something."

Me: "I thought I should try and lose weight before my bar mitzvah. You know, I have to get up in front of all those people and —"

Mom: "I remember your brother's bar mitzvah. He was so handsome, and he did such a nice job. Everyone kept telling me what a good boy he was. I was so proud."

Layne the Favorite beamed. I ate more monkfish. My appetite disappeared.

Week 2: Down four pounds.

***

IT RAINED THE next day. I came home in time for dinner soaking wet and out of breath from my run. I thought I had stumbled into the wrong house. It smelled like hot oil, bread crumbs, and a chicken that had died happy.

Me: "Oh my God! What are you doing?"

Mom: "I'm frying chicken."

Me: "I didn't know you could."

Mom: "What is wrong with you? Any shiksa can fry a chicken. I got the recipe from The Froog."

She was referring to The Frugal Gourmet, a cooking show that ran from 1983-1997 on PBS. Jeff Smith, the host, was a former minister turned chef.

Me: "But he's the king of the goyim! You watch the Frugal Gourmet?"

Mom: "All the time."

Me: "With the sound on?"

Mom: "Dinner will be ready in a few minutes." The oil popped. My mother winced. "It better be good. I don't understand why goyim want to hurt themselves to make food."

Me: "Better than hurting themselves by eating it."

Mom: "I never know what you're talking about. You're dripping water on my floor."

The chicken tasted like...well, like someone else had made it. I ate until I couldn't move. In future, desperate years, I asked for the Froog's Chicken. Never got it.

***

I APPROACHED MY house at a slow, wheezing jog. I was up to two miles a day and felt like I had been beat up by a big woman that I was too slow to run away from. My house was two blocks away; I set my sights on it and saw a huge plume of black smoke rising into the air.

Gasping like a beached whale, I ran faster.

***

MY MOTHER AND Ted the Drug Dealer were in the side yard, tears streaming from their eyes. Plumes of black smoke billowed from a hibachi grill.

Mom: "Ted. What is it with you and setting things on fire?"

Ted the Drug Dealer had set himself on fire once in Texas three years ago. For my mother, this was a trend. She had had it with his arsonist tendencies.

Ted the Drug Dealer: "I don't think you were supposed to use half a bottle of lighter fluid."

Mom: "Ted. How else was I supposed to start the goddamned fire?"

Ted the Drug Dealer: "I think if we just wait for it to burn off, we'll have hot coals we can cook over."

Me: "Dear God. Cook *what*?"

Mom: "Hamburgers."

I was stunned. Through the cloud of smoke I could see a plate of formed ground meat patties, yellow cheese, and buns.

Me: "What kind of meat is that?"

Mom: "Beef."

Me: "From a cow."

Mom: "Of course, from a cow. Where else would beef come from?"

Me: "And the cheese. Soy? Penguin? Aardvark? Desert sloth?"

Mom: "Also from a cow. You know, SSSStace, everyone tells me how smart you are. I'm not so sure..."

Me: "Where are the red onions? Where?"

Mom: "Onions on a hamburger? I'm not sure that would taste good."

Me: "Are you kidding me? You put red onions on apple pie! Did you fall down and hit your head or something?"

Mom: "Listen, Buster. I think you need to go lay down and take a nap. And you're not allowed to go jogging anymore. It's throwing your cells out of whack."

Me: "Cheeseburgers aren't kosher!"

Mom: "SSSSSSo. You take nineteen bar mitzvah classes and all of a sudden you're a Talmudic scholar?"

That night we had cheeseburgers. Swear to God. They were great. My cells really must have been out of whack.

***

I DIDN'T JOG the next day, as ordered. When I got home from school, I smelled tomato sauce. And frying meat. My mother stood before a stove with all the burners going. There was also something in the oven.

Me: "What's that?"

Mom: "I'm making spaghetti and meatballs."

Me: "You know what that is?"

Mom: "The Froog, Stace. Froog! You know what your problem is? You never listen."

Me: "Meat is a loose term around here. What kind of meat is it?"

Mom: "Beef. From a cow. Disgusting."

Me: "So why are you making it?"

Mom: "Because you like it."

Me: "Am I dying?"

Mom: "What are you talking about? Also there's garlic bread."

I fell back against the refrigerator and took a few deep breaths. Maybe I was dying. Or I was already dead. I always suspected Hell would look a lot like my mother's kitchen.

Me: "What kind of pasta? Spinach? Carrot? Rutabaga? Parsnip? Beet?"

Mom: "SSSStace. You sound like a crazy person. It's Ronzoni. Same crap as your goyim friends eat."

I ate two plates of spaghetti, forty meatballs, and a whole loaf of garlic bread.

***

MY MOTHER SPENT the next two weeks cooking all the Froog's favorites – sloppy joes, barbecued ribs, meatloaf. White flour and cheese made from cow's milk lived in our house, returned as if from a long exile.

Me: "Why did you wait my whole life to do this? Are you sure I'm not dying?"

Mom: "When it's your time to go it's your time to go."

Me: "Oh, right."

Mom: "Don't forget, Buster. We have to go get you measured for your bar mitzvah suit tomorrow."

Me: "Oh, heck!" I ran to the scale and weighed myself.

I had gained sixteen pounds. From my mother's cooking. Omar the Tentmaker hung his shingle back out.

20

TOP OF THE TRIANGLE

We Jews are great at building pyramids, but we always do it for someone else. You would think that with all the sandy misery that followed our enslavement, and after being cast out to wander the world for the next three thousand years, we would have finally learned what happens when we build pointy things for the Goyim.

Nope. Not even close.

***

My mother and Ted the Drug Dealer sat at the kitchen table. It was covered in papers and charts and loose leaf binders. There were small round jars of some kind of cream in a pile in one corner. My mother had threatened to serve us salmon and green beans for dinner, which tasted like being alone in a small boat lost at sea, but there were no horrific smells, no seething fish or oniony beans. Maybe she was serving paper with a nice cream sauce.

Me: "What's going on?"

Mom: "SSSSSSStace. We're starting a businesssssss."

Well. We had been here before.

***

TED THE LIGHTBULB Salesman stopped selling light bulbs three months after we made it to California. We lived in a trailer park, and although he was required to wear a suit and tie every day, he longed to sport flip flops and a t-shirt. He glided past the other men of the trailer park, fancy and overdressed each morning, but all he wanted was to be like them. The sales job, with its expense accounts, quarterly bonuses, and martini lunches wasn't going to cut it anymore. He was trailer trash.

Once unemployed, he began the search for a new career. The only things he had ever been good at were uprooting us from everything we had ever known, flinging us across the country to live in a box, and setting things on fire. He would have a great future as a travel agent, or those guys in Hawaii who spit fire from their mouths. Unfortunately, there was no way we could get the RV to Hawaii.

The night he quit his job, we sat around the small fold down table in the camper, choking on my mother's turkey and cauliflower stew, which made me think of being trapped underground while the air ran out, because the noxious steamed mess seemed to suck the oxygen out of the room. My mother was already light-headed, having succumbed to her self-inflicted arsenic poisoning.

Ted the Idle: "As you know, I need a job."

Mom: "Ted. Of course you need a goddamned job. You're not going to sit around here all day and do nothing."

Me (hopefully): "He could take over the shopping and the cooking!"

Layne the Favorite: "My mother is the best cook ever." He ate some cauliflower. His eyes watered. He poked at some boiled turkey with his fork and gritted his teeth.

Ted the Idle: "I had an interesting meeting today. Very interesting." He took a bite of turkey stew, gasped, and laid out the plan.

***

THESE WERE THE days when selling things door to door was in vogue: life insurance, vacuum cleaners, encyclopedias, and magazine subscriptions, to name a few. Ted the Idle met with a fellow who would sell him, on a commission basis, a territory in the San Diego area that he could plunder to sell magazine subscriptions. As time went on and Ted became successful, he could buy into more areas and recruit other people to run his former territories for him. The man who recruited him only got 75 percent of Ted's net profit. As Ted signed up underlings, he would get 75 percent of their net. The man above him got 75 percent of that.

Me: "It's a pyramid scheme."

Mom: "It is not!"

Ted the Idle: "How would you know anyway? You're just a kid."

Oh, really? Game on, Ted. Game on.

***

I ARRANGED THE gelatinous pieces of turkey and cauliflower on my plate. The base consisted of four oozing turkey chunks. On top of that, I placed three pieces of shriveled cauliflower and then two more pieces of turkey. Carefully, I positioned one lump of cauliflower at the peak of my pyramid. It looked like a drippy brain. This was probably the most useful my mother's food had ever been. I gestured at the cauliflower on the top:

Me: "This is the guy you met with." Ted the Idle nodded.

Me (pointing at one of the hunks of turkey below it): "This is you."

Ted the Idle: "Actually, I think I'm the other one. It looks less slimy."

Me: "It's good to aspire. So the cauliflower takes 75 percent of what you and the other turkey produce, right?"

Ted the Idle gave me a thumbs up.

I poked the cauliflower below.

Me: "You recruit these vegetables to sell for you, and you keep 75 percent of their take."

Ted the Idle beamed. He nodded smugly.

Me: "Of which King Cauliflower takes 75 percent."

Ted the Idle: "Yes."

Me: "It's a pyramid."

Mom: "SSSSSSStace. It's a triangle. Look at it! What is *wrong* with you?"

Layne the Favorite: "Definitely a triangle. Guess you're not so smart, are you, smart guy?"

Ted the Idle: "I'll make a *fortune*."

Getting us to build pyramids for free was probably a cake walk for the ancient Egyptians.

Ancient Egyptian Overseer (drawing in the sand): "You just stack the bricks, then assemble fewer on top. In fact, it gets easier as you go up."

Ted the Israelite: "Why's that?"

Ancient Egyptian Overseer: "Less bricks."

Ted the Israelite: "What's this called again?"

Ancient Egyptian Overseer (proudly): "A pyramid."

Ted the Israelite: "That's a stupid name for it. It's a triangle. Look at it!"

Ancient Egyptian Overseer: "Whatever you say. Let me show you and your friends where the bricks are."

Ted the Israelite: "This is gonna be *great!*"

It was not. We had to turn their rivers to blood, send locusts raining down on their heads, and part a sea to get out of that gig. When Ted the Mobile Magazine Seller finally ended his career, he owed King Cauliflower thirteen thousand dollars.

***

MY PARENTS SAT at the table, surrounded by colorful paper charts and jars of cream. They looked triumphant.

Me: "So you're selling this cream now?"

STACEY ROBERTS

Mom: "SSSSStace. It's not cream. It's *product*."

Me: "In cream form."

Mom: "I'm not following."

Me: "What does it do?"

There were three kinds of cream: the Tightener, the Melter, and Creamed Bullshit. The Tightener was a —

Mom: "SSSSStace. It's not a tightener. What the *product* does is constrict your pores. It shrinks the cells. It's a lift!"

Me: "What does it lift?"

Mom: "Everything. Forehead, lips, bust, tush. Everything. You know what? You could sell the *product* to your little friends' mothers! I bet they need their tushes lifted."

Me: "I'm sure they'll be glad to hear that."

The Melter was a cream that had to be applied vigorously to flabby body areas, which were then— "

Mom: "What is *wrong* with you? It's called Body Wrap. What it does, Buster, is it reacts with your flab cells to create a reaction. Then we wrap you in Cleansing Film —"

Uh oh. This sounded like cooking. Not her strong suit.

The idea was to coat flabby areas - hips, tush, belly, thighs - in the Melter —"

Mom: "Body Wrap!"

—and then wrap the offending areas in saran wrap. In just a few hours, women (and men) could lose inches of flab.

Creamed Bullshit was a miracle potion that promised to fix damn near anything, as long as you covered yourself in it completely before you went to bed. At that rate, you could run through a case of Creamed Bullshit a week. It was a great scam, because —

Mom: "Scam? This is no scam! The Rejuvenator (Creamed Bullshit) is like a fountain of youth! You put it on and it will make you younger! You know how, smart guy? It rebuilds your cells. Your cells!"

You could also buy special pads for your bed so that, once coated head to toe in Creamed Bullshit, you wouldn't slide around like a pat of butter in a hot pan.

Mom: "Butter kills your cells."

Me: "Which is why we coat ourselves in Creamed Bullshit."

Mom: "Rejuvenator, SSSStace! Rejuvenator!"

We had a hundred of these pads in the garage. Louise had let them go for fourteen thousand dollars. They were yoga mats. We could have gotten them for a tenth of the price at Walmart. Louise did.

✳✳✳

MY MOTHER AND Ted the Drug Dealer explained the system:

They bought the cream —

Mom: "*Product!*"

—from Louise, who was a Golden Distributor.

Mom: "Her name's Lisa. Liza. Lana?"

Ted the Drug Dealer: "I'm pretty sure it's Louise. That's what it says on her business card."

Mom: "That's what I said."

Their initial investment was about eighteen thousand dollars. We had cases and cases of Tightener, Melter, and Creamed Bullshit all over the house. As they sold the product, 50 percent of their profits went to Louise. As they ran out of cream, they bought more from Louise, who was buying it from the Platinum Distributor above her, whom she paid 40 percent of her profits. My mother and Ted the Drug Dealer were Silver Distributors. They could in turn recruit Bronze Distributors below them, who then—

Me: "It's a pyramid scheme."

Mom: "No it isn't."

I took the jars of cream from the boxes lined up on the floor and cleared a space on the kitchen room table. Then I lined up four jars of Tightener cream.

Mom: "*Not* cream! *Product*! And it's a lift!"

Me: "So these are the Bronze Distributors." I took three jars of Melter and stacked them on top of the bottom row. Our mummified Egyptian overseers looked up from the Realm of Osiris with approval.

Me: "These are the Silver Distributors."

Mom: "That's us!"

I took two jars of Tightener and put them on top.

Me: "Golden Distributors."

Mom: "Lola says that once we hit four hundred thousand dollars of product, we could become Golden Distributors."

Me: "Or homeowners."

Mom: "What?"

Me: "Never mind." I took a jar of Creamed Bullshit and put it at the apex of the pyramid.

Me: "Platinum Distributor."

Mom: "Right!"

Me: "It's a pyramid."

Mom: "SSSSSStace. It's a *triangle*."

Ted the Drug Dealer: "We're going to make a *fortune*."

***

THE PATH TO riches was paved with a plan: my mother would rent a conference room at a hotel, bring a truckload of cream (*product!*) and invite women in need of tushie lifting, face smoothing, and cell rejuvenation to show up for some Creamed Bullshit.

Because I was only twelve, I could not be left home alone. Layne the Favorite, at fourteen, was perfectly capable of staying home on Saturday, watching cartoons, eating all the snacks in the house, and doing whatever else he wanted.

Me: "Can't Layne watch me?"

Mom: "No way, Buster. Your brother needs his alone time. Do you have any idea how taxing it is to spend a day with you?"

Me: "I guess we're about to find out."

***

WE LOADED UP a van my mother had bought (the Creammobile) —

Mom: "*Product*! *Product*mobile!"

—with cases and cases of expensive unguents and drove them to the conference center, which, inexplicably, was ninety miles away. My job was to unload the *product* into the conference room, open boxes of Tightener, Melter, and Creamed Bullshit, and arrange them on a specialized display that my mother had bought from Louise for five hundred dollars.

Mom: "SSSStace. It displays the *product*. The *product*!"

Me: "You could hire someone to stand there and hold it at every show for five hundred bucks."

Mom: "Are you volunteering?"

She had me there.

***

FLABBY AUDIENCE MEMBER: "So if I cover my love handles in this Melter Cream —"

Mom: "Body Wrap."

Flabby Audience Member: "I'll lose inches?"

Mom: "Yesss. Once we wrap you in the Cleansing Film."

My mother had bought boxes and boxes of Cleansing Film from Louise at forty dollars a box. It could be had at any local grocery store for a dollar a package. Because it was saran wrap.

***

THE CONFERENCE ROOM deteriorated into a kind of hellish Peter Paul Rubens painting from the 17th century: large women had stripped down to their bras and panties and were smearing each other with globs of Melter while my mother shouted at them:

Mom: "Carla! You've got to cover your whole tush!"

Cathy: "Cathy."

Mom: "That's what I said. If you can't reach the whole zaftig thing, get Martha to help you."

Melissa: "My name's not Martha."

Mom: "That doesn't matter right now. Take some Body Wrap and shmear it on Connie's tush."

Mom: "SSSSStace. Get the Cleansing Film and go over there and wrap Christie's love handles."

I bolted past groups of smeared women. They stared at me as I fled screaming from the room.

***

THE MIRACLE CREAM business worked out as expected. At the end of it, my mother and Ted the Drug Dealer owed their Golden Distributor forty nine thousand dollars in overrides. Since they couldn't pay, Louise had to settle for repossessing the Creammobile.

She wouldn't even take back the hundreds of cases of unused *product*. To this day, when I go to visit my mother, I look in the closet in her spare bedroom, the kitchen pantry, and the garage.

I can always find a few jars of Creamed Bullshit.

AFTERWORD

By Stacey's Mom

SSSSSSo. Now HE's writing books. That's nice. He asked me to write a blurb to go with this load of *chazerai*. I don't get what kind of book this is supposed to be. It's nothing like that Diana Steele. Daisy? Doreen? Something like that. I really like her books. If he could write like that, maybe he could take care of his mother in her old age. So Stacey thinks he's the newest Joe Grisham. Josh? Jimmy? Whatever. He wants me to write a page or two. Like I work for him all of a sudden.

"I never heard of this, this blurb," I told him. "It sounds Yiddish."

He said to read the book, and then write whatever popped into my head.

"What is *wrong* with you?" I asked him. "How could I write something that *didn't* pop into my head?"

SSSSSSo. I read these "stories" of his, and listen, Busters, most of it isn't true. He likes lists so much, I'll make one for you. How do you like that?

1. Let me tell you something: there's nothing wrong with my cooking. All these comparisons he makes to my food tasting like despair, grief, and all that *chazerai* is nonsense. Look at him! Would he be so *zaftig* if my food was no good?

2. You know what his problem is? He likes the *shiksas* with big boobs. All they do is cook for him with grease, sugar, salt, white flour, cheese, and bacon. They put gravy on everything, the *shiksas*. You know what that does to your cells? And eating all that goyisher food? He's as Jewish as George W. Bush! Disgusssting.

3. Layner never complained about my food. He's such a good boy.

4. Smoking has nothing to do with low birth weight. He was a preemie because he didn't form right. He didn't have any lungs. I was sure he was gonna die.

5. Stacey is not a girl's name. What about Stacy Keach? What about him? He's not a girl! I kept telling him. Did he listen? No.

6. Living in the RV was not some kind of prison sentence. You know where he gets this flair for the dramatic? His father. He's just like him. If I told Fred once, I told him a hundred times. I said, "Fred. You're a real son of a bitch. You know that?"

7. Ted was no drug dealer. He got arrested for selling a silencer. A *silencer*. And he was set up. The only thing wrong with Ted was that he kept setting things on fire.

8. Onions are good for you. They open up your capillaries. Nothing else does that. You want to have capillary problems? Fine by me.

9. I remember *everybody's* names. Take Ssssstace's ex-wife, Kim. She's absolutely wonderful. I call her every week and we talk for hours. We have so much in common. I mean, she's another one of those *shiksas* with the boobs, but she's not impressed at all by his smart-aleckyness. Not one bit, let me tell you. She really should have married Layner instead.

10. Layner is *not* my favorite. I love both of my sons equally. If SSSSSStace could have been more like his brother, he would have had a happier childhood. Layne's such a good boy. He would never make up these kinds of *facochta* stories about his mother.

And, he thinks he's funny. Let me tell you something: there's nothing funny about arsenic poisoning. Smart Guy's laughing while my hair falls out and I lose my train of thought? Is that supposed to be —?

Oh, hell. I forgot what I was talking about. Doesn't matter.

And another thing. Living in an RV was an experience. You hear me? We traveled the whole country. So what if we had a few mechanical problems? And almost running straight into Hoover Dam? Big deal. When it's your time to go, it's your time to go.

When I retire, I'm buying a motor home and traveling around. I'll stop at each of my relatives for a few months and park in their goddamned driveways.

My son, the writer? He's first.

COMING IN SUMMER, 2014:
THE FALL OF TED THE DRUG DEALER

THE TRAILER TRASH saga continues. Read the next chapter of a life on wheels gone bad when Ted's career as a furtive criminal comes to an end after a grieving police detective brings him down. It's got attack dogs, weapons, drunkards, sea captains, and a hair dryer. Sometimes what happens in the Winnebago...should stay in the Winnebago...

Ted the Marijuana Farmer

WHEN I WAS fifteen, Ted the Drug Dealer drove his cab to Kentucky, killed a dog with a machete, and brought home four hundred pounds of marijuana.

The rumor was that police departments in Central and Western Kentucky, as part of their war on drugs, had confiscated whole marijuana fields. This was big news to Ted the Drug Dealer and his Council of Advisors, a small group of fellows who met regularly at our house.

The group only convened at night, around our kitchen table. There was Tiny, a heroin addict who weighed nearly six hundred pounds. Ted the Drug Dealer supplied him with methadone for heroin withdrawal. He also provided him with heroin for heroin withdrawal; Tiny was a waddling contradiction. It was a good thing we didn't still live in the

Winnebago; Tiny would not have fit through the door. He didn't sit on our kitchen chairs, instead, he leaned against the wall.

Louie the Cokehead was also on the Council. He was a real-estate agent who was a year away from being convicted of embezzling his clients' escrow funds and down payments to support his ever growing habit.

Rounding out the foursome was Marty the Stoner, a college boy from the University of Miami that Ted the Drug Dealer had picked up from the airport once in his cab. Even though Marty was twenty years younger, he and Ted had hit it off.

My mother offered to cook for them, but they always declined.

Mom: "I can't believe you're turning down food, Tony. How about a salad?"

Tiny: "Oh, no, Carol. I don't like red onions. And it's Tiny."

Mom: "This salad is perfectly big enough for one person. And red onions are good for your circulation."

Tiny: "I mean my *name* is Tiny. I tell you every time I come here."

Mom: "That's what I said."

It was Marty the Stoner who brought the news of the pot fields in Kentucky to the meeting. He was the intellectual of the group, being of academia.

Louie the Cokehead: "They burn those fields, Marty."

Marty the Stoner: "Nope. They're keeping them intact."

Tiny: "Why would they do that?"

Marty the Stoner: "To sell the pot. To use it to rope in dealers. Whatever. All I know is that the cops have weed fields up there with no protection."

Ted the Drug Dealer: "We should go get us some. How soon can we leave?"

Tiny: "I can't leave the county, let alone the state." His large baby face turned a deeper red. "It's a condition of my treatment."

Louie the Cokehead: "I've got a meeting Monday with some regulators from the real estate licensing board. I could go next weekend though."

Actually, he couldn't. The regulators turned out to be just the first meeting of many that would result in his arrest. By the following weekend he would be in jail, calling Ted the Drug Dealer with his one phone call, begging for a fix.

My mother took that call.

Mom: "Who is this?"

Louie the Cokehead: "It's Louie, Carol. Is Ted there?"

Mom: "Lenny. Ted's in Kansas."

Louie the Cokehead: "What's he doing there?"

Mom: "Larry. He went to get the pot! You forgot already? The pot!"

Louie the Cokehead: "The pot's in Kentucky, Carol."

Mom: "Lance. That's what I said."

Louie the Cokehead: "Did Ted leave anything for me while he's out of town?"

Mom: "Oh, hell, Leo. I got no idea where he keeps your crap. I'll tell him when he gets back."

Louie the Cokehead: "When's he coming back?"

Mom: "I don't know what you need that for, Leonard. Take a multi."

Louie the Cokehead: "A what?"

Mom: "A multi, Laslo. A multivitamin!"

She hung up. That was Louie the Cokehead's one phone call.

✳✳✳

TED THE DRUG Dealer looked around at his Council of Advisors. Tiny and Louie the Cokehead were not going with him. Marty the Stoner was all he had left.

Marty the Stoner: "Ted, dude, I got this paper due in Economics that's kicking my ass, man."

Ted the Drug Dealer: "So I have to do this myself?"

Marty the Stoner: "Bro, I promise. I can move whatever you bring back."

Me: "I'll go."

Ted the Drug Dealer: "Your mother won't let you."

Me: "She won't even know I'm gone."

Ted the Drug Dealer: "What will we tell the school?"

Me: "Field trip? Literally?"

Louie the Cokehead: "Ted, you can't take him with you. He's just a kid."

Me: "I'm smarter than *you*, Louie."

Louie the Cokehead: "I'm smart enough to stay out of trouble with the law."

He had me there. For about another week.

Ted the Drug Dealer: "You better stay here."

***

HE WENT ALONE, driving up on a Thursday (the drive from South Florida was about fifteen hours). A fraternity brother of Marty the Stoner's from Western Kentucky University supplied the location of the field. Ted spent Friday finding it, then went in after midnight on Saturday morning to do the harvest. He told the story to his reduced Council of Advisors upon his return, after a few housekeeping items.

Ted the Drug Dealer: "I think we should pass the plate around and send something to Louie."

Louie's cocaine withdrawal in jail had gotten so bad, he had been admitted to the hospital under guard. They let him have another phone call once he was in his room, so he called my mother again.

Louie the Cokehead: "Carol, it's Louie."

Mom: "Ted's not here, Linus. He's in California."

Louie the Cokehead: "Son of a bitch! What's he doing in California?"

Mom: "Landon. What the hell is wrong with you? He went to get the pot!"

Louie the Cokehead: "Goddamn it, Carol! The pot is in Kentucky!"

Louie the Cokehead's Jail Guard: "Pot? What are you talking about? What pot? Gimme the phone. Who is this?"

Mom: "Who is *this*?"

Louie the Cokehead's Jail Guard: "Mr. Lippert is under arrest. He's under guard at Hollywood Memorial Hospital."

Mom: "He should have taken a multi."

Louie the Cokehead's Jail Guard: "A what, ma'am?"

Mom (gritting her teeth): "A multi! *Multeeeeeeeee!* What is *wrong* with you? How could you not know that?"

She hung up.

***

TED THE DRUG Dealer stared down his Council of Advisors. "Nothing for Louie?"

Tiny: "Well, Ted, I think what he wants is a big bucket of cocaine. I can't help - I'm on probation."

Me: "Or what, Tiny? You mean if you weren't, you'd take Louie a bucket of cocaine to the hospital where he's under police guard?"

Marty the Stoner: "I think we're getting off topic." He licked his lips. "Tell us about the pot, Ted."

* * *

TED THE DRUG Dealer sat in his cold, dark cab, parked at the end of a dirt road in Kentucky. He shivered; he had lived too long in tropical climates, and he did not own a coat. His machete was gripped in his right hand and he had black garbage bags tied around his waist. The food my mother had packed him sat uneaten on the passenger seat, reeking of decayed critter, red onions, and despair.

He got out of the car at four in the morning. In the rural darkness, the cab's interior light was as bright as a searchlight. Startled, Ted flailed around with the machete, smashing the plastic dome. He sat in the dark while he waited for his eyes to adjust. Once he could see again, he started for the fields, alone, silent, and armed only with a machete. Generations of ancient dead warriors approved, and were rooting for him. He could feel it.

* * *

TWO HOURS LATER, he had stripped his shirt off and was covered in sweat, hacking away at marijuana plants and stuffing them in garbage bags. With each full one, he had to drag it back to the trunk of the cab. It was hot, miserable work.

He was out in a fresh section of the field, swinging away, filling the bag, when he heard the dogs approaching. There were two Dobermans, sleek and mad. He thought for a second about the pistol he had left in the cab, then swung the machete, killing the first dog. The second locked its teeth on the leg of his jeans. He screamed like a little girl in a sundress with a frilly hat, wet himself, and fled for the safety of the cab, the second dog at his heels.

Ted the Drug Dealer didn't mention his "accident", but he did not do his own laundry. The shredded, urine-stained jeans were noticed by my mother, who handled it with her usual diplomacy:

Mom: "Ted. These pants are ruined. They're ripped. And they smell funny. Disgusting."

She shoved them under his nose. Her own sense of smell had been ruined by the arsenic poisoning she got from not washing vegetables when we lived in California. Everything smelled funny to her. These particular pants reeked of panicked urine.

Ted the Drug Dealer: "Just throw them out."

***

TED MADE IT to the cab. First, he secured the marijuana, which cost him precious time. The Doberman was on him as soon as he closed the trunk. He kicked it away and climbed in the front seat. The dog jumped up at him, fouling the closed window with slimy drool.

Ted the Drug Dealer, afraid that the sound of the barking would alert someone, resolved to get back out of the cab and kill the dog with his machete. He gritted his teeth, gripped his weapon, and was ready to open the door when he saw the food my mother had sent with him. It was a thick sandwich: slabs of meat Mom called "turkey," half of a red onion, stacks of lettuce, two wet slices of mealy tomato, and soy-based mayonnaise, all stuffed between two pieces of bread made from coarsely ground beet flour. It was a purple, smelly mess. Unwrapping

TRAILER TRASH, WITH A GIRL'S NAME

it made his eyes water, but the stench eclipsed the rising tide of urine, which was slightly better. He flung himself across the seat to the passenger side, rolled down the window, and chucked the sandwich over the roof of the cab. It landed behind the remaining guard dog, who spun around, ran for it, and gobbled it up. Ted started the cab and screamed away.

The dog finished the sandwich and stared after Ted's disappearing cab. It took a few halfhearted steps in pursuit, then lay down in the middle of the dirt path, its insides in complete upheaval. The dog moaned miserably, hacked a few bitter coughs, and slowly crawled into the marijuana field, where the police found it dead the next morning. There were no marks on it.

*** *** ***

THE MARIJUANA WAS unloaded into the house. At first, it was stacked in my parents' bedroom. My mother got tired of that after one night.

Mom: "Ted. That crap smells like rotten spinach."

Ted the Drug Dealer: "How would you know?"

Mom: "Just get it out of here."

The next day we moved it into the kitchen. Ted the Drug Dealer knew he had to dry it out before he could sell it, so he stuffed the buds into the oven. We all sat around the table and waited.

Layne the Favorite: "It smells terrible."

Mom: "It's okay, Layner. It's only for a little while."

Me: "Can you smell it?"

Mom: "SSSSSSStace. What is wrong with you? You know I can't smell anything. I got the arsenic poisoning. You forgot? The arsenic! It killed the cells in my nostrils."

Me: "Cells regenerate."

Mom: "Not when they're blasted by arsssssenic. There's no coming back from that."

Ted the Drug Dealer: "I'm hungry."

Mom: "I made a soup from that turkey carcass. The same one I used to make the sandwiches for your trip. It's in the fridge near the onions."

Ted the Drug Dealer: "Everything in that fridge is near the onions." The contact high he was getting from the baking pot was lowering his inhibitions.

Mom: "What are you talking about? Just eat the soup."

Ted the Drug Dealer brought the container to the table. The soup was a gelatinous cube of brown. Onions, carrots, and celery poked through the surface. The turkey bones were at the dark center of the cube like a diseased heart. Despite the heat of the oven, we all felt a cold chill, as if the ghost of a dead Kentucky dog had come into the kitchen.

Ted the Drug Dealer: "The oven's not working." He got up from the table and shut it off.

* * *

MARTY THE STONER was called in for a consult. He assessed the situation and then, with the crisp authority of a surgeon, called for a hammer, nails, clothesline, and clothespins.

We spent the next few hours stringing clothesline the length of the kitchen and living room. When we finished, a dozen hung throughout the house. Marty the Stoner showed us the proper way to hang the branches upside down, so the fan leaves covered the buds. He warned us against mold and mildew, and promised to come back in two to six weeks for phase two.

Ted the Drug Dealer: "Phase two?"

Mom: "Two to six weeks?"

Marty the Stoner explained that the plants had to dry, then be put in paper bags so the seeds would dry. After that, they were to be cured in jars.

Marty the Stoner looked at me. "Can you keep an eye on these plants, little dude? Make sure they don't get mold on them. Then you can be in charge of them while they're in the paper bags."

My life of crime was off to a great start.

✳✳✳

I TENDED TO the marijuana plants for the next several days. I wasn't sure what mold or mildew looked like, but I kept an eye out.

Saturday morning, my friend Mark called. He was supposed to come over to work on our World History project. We were in the model United Nations – I was the United States and he was Libya. We decided to team up and put forth some joint resolutions before the model General Assembly.

My mother heard the tail end of my phone call with Mark and rushed through the hanging marijuana at top speed, like an Amazon jaguar with no sense of smell.

Mom: "SSSSSStace. What is wrong with you? Martin can't come over."

Me: "Mark."

Mom: "That's what I said. He can't come here."

Me: "Why not?"

Mom (gritting her teeth): "SSSSSSStace. Look around. There's pot hanging everywhere! What is wrong with your eyes?"

Me: "Arsenic poisoning?"

Mom: "You're just like your father. Moe can't come to the god-damned house. Because of the pot!"

Me: "He won't mind."

Mom: "No way! He can't come over!"

Me (to Mark on the phone): "You can't come over."

Mark: "Okay."

Mom: "Don't tell him why!"

Me: "There's pot strung up on clotheslines here."

***

By Monday of the following week, Layne the Favorite had had enough:

Layne the Favorite: "I have had enough!"

Mom: "Layner, what's wrong?"

Layne the Favorite: "This crap has to go! I hate that it's hanging in our house. Ted's going to have to get rid of it."

Mom: "Okay, honey."

***

MARTY THE STONER slammed the trunk of his car closed. He tried to look sorrowful as he handed Ted the Drug Dealer four hundred dollars in damp, wrinkled cash.

Marty the Stoner: "I feel for you, man."

Ted could not speak. He glumly pocketed the money and looked at the trunk of Marty's car.

Marty the Stoner: "I mean, dude, that dog could have killed you."

Ted the Drug Dealer nodded.

Marty the Stoner: "You coulda gotten pulled over by the cops. That much pot is a pretty hefty prison sentence."

Ted the Drug Dealer looked at his own shoes, his arms crossed over his chest.

Marty the Stoner: "And Carol said you wet your pants."

Ted the Drug Dealer: "What?"

Marty the Stoner: "All for nothing."

Ted the Drug Dealer thought about pulling his pistol and shooting Marty the Stoner between the eyes.

Marty the Stoner: "Because your wife didn't want the pot in her house for a few weeks. That's why I'm not getting married, man. Ever."

Ted the Drug Dealer: "It wasn't her. It was her son. The favorite."

Marty the Stoner: "That's why I'm not having kids, dude."

Layne the Favorite watched from the kitchen window, a small smile on his face. Ted the Drug Dealer had no chance at all.

***

I WAS PUTTING out the trash when Marty the Stoner drove away. I watched Ted the Drug Dealer walk dejectedly back into the house. Layne the Favorite's head disappeared from the kitchen window before Ted made it inside.

A brown Ford sedan idled slowly down our street and parked directly across from our house. There was a balding man in his early sixties at the wheel. He had a face like a basset hound. He stared mournfully at Ted the Drug Dealer as he made his way inside. He sat in his car in the Florida heat just watching the house for another hour before driving off.

Somehow I knew we'd be seeing him again...

ABOUT THE AUTHOR

STACEY ROBERTS WAS born in a smoky hospital in New Jersey in 1971. Nine years later, he and his family moved into a Winnebago and traveled across the country. After several near-death experiences, they settled first in California and then Florida.

He attended college at Florida State University and University of Miami, where he received his B.A. in English Literarature instead of Finance, which was a great disappointment to his mother.

He went on to get a Master's degree in Early Modern European History at the University of Cincinnati, to which his mother said, "SSSStace. History? What do you need that for? What is *wrong* with you?"

His mother was right. He didn't need it for anything, except to make arcane references to the Roman Empire or Henry VIII that no one else understands.

He founded a computer consulting firm outside of Cincinnati, Ohio in 1994 and resides in Northern Kentucky with his two brilliant daughters and their less-than-brilliant yellow dog Sophie.

Trailer Trash, With a Girl's Name is his first novel.

Made in the USA
Charleston, SC
21 March 2014